Bush Theatre

SPEED
by Mohamed-Zain Dada

Speed premiered at the Bush Theatre, London,
on 4 April 2025.

SPEED
by Mohamed-Zain Dada

Cast
Faiza — Shazia Nicholls
Samir — Arian Nik
Abz — Nikesh Patel
Harleen — Sabrina Sandhu

Creative Team
Director — Milli Bhatia
Set & Costume Designer — Tomás Palmer
Lighting Designer — Jessica Hung Han Yun
Sound Designer & Composer — XANA
Movement Director — Theophilus O. Bailey
Fight Director — Bret Yount
Costume Supervisor — Beth Qualter Buncall
Associate Lighting Designer & Programmer — Stephen Settle
Production Dramatherapy — Wabriya King
Casting Director — Arthur Carrington
Video Asset Designers — DMLK Video

Production Manager — Adam Jefferys
Associate Production Manager — Jordan Harris
Company Stage Manager — Stacey Nurse
Assistant Stage Manager — Alexander Standish-Murray

Set Builder — Centre Stage Scenery
Production Electrician — Kevin James
Production Carpenter — Ben Jones

For the Bush
Lead Producer — Nikita Karia
Dramaturg — Titilola Dawudu
Resident Director — Katie Greenall
Marketing Campaign Lead — Kelly Thurston
Technical Manager — Jamie Haigh
Schools Project Lead & Community Producer — Holly Smith

This production is generously supported by Charles Holloway OBE.

Cast

Shazia Nicholls | Faiza

Shazia has just finished performing as Mrs Quickly in *The Merry Wives of Windsor* directed by Blanche McIntyre for the Royal Shakespeare Company. Before arriving in Stratford, Shazia starred in *The Duchess of Malfi* for the Globe at the Sam Wanamker Playhouse and *The Inquiry* at Chichester Festival Theatre. Screenwise, Shazia recently wrapped Alfonso Cuarón's latest series *Disclaimer* for AppleTV+ opposite Cate Blanchett and HeYeon Jung. Prior to this, Shazia was on stage in Margaret Perry's Olivier award-nominated play *Paradise Now!* at the Bush theatre. She can be seen in Peter Kosminsky's *Darkness Rising* as well as *Call the Midwife* for the BBC. She is perhaps best known for her role in the critically acclaimed series *Dr Foster* opposite Suranne Jones. Other credits include the National Theatre's *Antony and Cleopatra*, *The Winter's Tale* and Lady Macbeth in *Macbeth*.

Arian Nik | Samir

Arian Nik trained at Mountview Academy.

Theatre credits includes: *Blue Mist* and *Sokhan Begoo* (Royal Court); *Kabul Goes Pop: Music Television Afghanistan* (Brixton House); and *The Village* (Stratford East).

TV and Film credits includes: *Daddy Issues* and *Film Club* (BBC); *Missing You* (Netflix); *Passenger* and *Count Abdulla* (ITV); *Giant* (AGC Studios); *Allelujah* (Pathé); and *Artemis Fowl* (Disney).

Nikesh Patel | Abz

Nikesh Patel stars in the upcoming Amazon feature film *Picture This* as Akshay, opposite Simone Ashley. He also recently starred in the second season of *The Devil's Hour* for Amazon. Other recent highlights include season three of the BBC/HBO hit show *Starstruck*, playing the lead role of Tom Kapoor opposite Rose Matefeo, and in the feature film *The Critic* directed by Anand Tucker.

Other highlights include Kash in Mindy Kaling's ten-part *Four Weddings and a Funeral* (Hulu) and Foaly in feature film *Artemis Fowl*, directed by Kenneth Branagh (Disney). Nikesh trained at the Guildhall School of Drama and was named as the 2010 Screen's UK Stars of Tomorrow.

Sabrina Sandhu | Harleen

Sabrina trained at the Television Workshop.

Her television credits include *The Syndicate* (BBC); Dodger (BBC/NBC Universal); *Maternal* (ITV) and the guest lead in *Not Going Out* (BBC). Most recently, she starred in the critically acclaimed *Dinosaur* (BBC/HULU) by Two Brothers, and the second series of the smash hit *We Are Lady Parts* (Working Title).

On stage, Sabrina's credits include Pritti Pasha in *Everybody's Talking About Jamie* at the Apollo in London's West End, *I Dare You* at the Nottingham Playhouse/Leicester Curve, *If We Were Older* for the National Theatre and *East Is East* for the Nottingham Playhouse.

Sabrina has worked on several projects for BBC Radio and won the Best Debut Performance award at the BBC Audio Drama Awards for her work on *Black Eyed Girls* (BBC Radio 4).

Creative Team

Mohamed-Zain Dada | Writer

Mohamed-Zain Dada goes by the name Zain and is a playwright and screenwriter. His first writing credit, *Emily (Glitched) In Paris*, was for the Royal Court Theatre's Living Newspaper series in March 2021. He is an alumnus of BBC Drama Room's 2022–23 cohort and NFTS x Left Bank Pictures inaugural Diverse Writer's Room Programme 2024. Zain's debut play, *Blue Mist*, premiered at the Jerwood Theatre Upstairs at the Royal Court Theatre in October 2023 to four- and five-star reviews and was nominated for an Olivier Award. His second play, *Dizzy*, premiered at the Sheffield Playhouse (co-produced by Theatre Centre).

Milli Bhatia | Director

Milli is a stage, screen and radio director, and dramaturg from East London. She is an Associate Artist at Synergy, and was Associate Director at the Royal Court Theatre.

Before this, she was Trainee Director and then Literary Associate at the Royal Court, Associate Artist at the Bush Theatre, Resident Assistant Director at Birmingham Rep and Creative Associate at the Gate Theatre. Her training includes the National Theatre Director's Programme, and the Old Vic 12.

She is a two-time Olivier Award nominee, for her productions of *seven methods of killing kylie jenner* and *Blue Mist*, both premiered at The Royal Court Theatre. She has also been nominated for Off West End Awards, Visionary Arts Awards, EE Awards and Asian Media Awards, and her work has received West End and international transfers, including to The Public Theater NYC, Woolly Mammoth DC, Riksteatern and The Swedish Biennale (Dramaten).

Her work in theatre also includes: *Chasing Hares* (Young Vic); *King Troll (The Fawn)* (New Diorama); *My White Best Friend and Other Letters Left Unsaid* (Royal Court/Bunker); *Macbeth: Something Wicked* (Donmar tour); *Liberation Squares* (Nottingham Playhouse/Brixton House/National tour); *Dismantle This Room* (Bush/Royal Court); and *Maryland* and *Baghdaddy* (Royal Court).

Tomás Palmer | Set and Costume Designer

Tomás trained at the Glasgow School of Art and the Royal Welsh College of Music and Drama. He is a recipient of the 2021 Linbury prize for theatre design and was the production designer on the Bafta award winning short film *Too Rough*.

As an artist, he has created installations/performance pieces for the Centre for Contemporary Arts (Glasgow), Transmission Gallery (Glasgow) and Embassy Gallery (Edinburgh).

Design credits include: *Wish You Were Here* (Gate); *Dawns y Ceirw* (Theatr Cymru, National Dance Company Wales); *Dreaming and Drowning* (Bush); *Blue Mist* (Royal Court); *The Bacchae* (The Lyric Hammersmith); *My Uncle Is Not Pablo Escobar* (Brixton House); *Sanctuary* (Access All Areas); *Sophocles' Oedipus/Silent Practice* (LAMDA); *Time Is Running Out* (Gate, Cardiff); *Winning* (Glasgow School of Art); *Autocue* (Centre for Contemporary Art Glasgow).

Costume design credits include: *Look Back In Anger*, *Roots* (Almeida); *Multiple Casualty Incident* (Yard); *Julius Caesar* (RSC).

Jessica Hung Han Yun | Lighting Designer

Theatre credits include: *Dr. Strangelove* (Noel Coward Theatre); *Fan Girls* (Lyric Hammersmith); *Alma Mater* (Almeida Theatre); *Withnail & I* (Birmingham Rep); *Lyonesse* (Harold Pinter Theatre); *My Neighbour Totoro* (West End/Royal Shakespeare Company/Barbican); *Little Shop of Horrors*, *Miss Saigon*, *The Good Person of Szechwan*, *The Band Plays On*, *She Loves Me*, *Reasons to Stay Alive* (Sheffield Theatres); *Wild Rose* (Lyceum Edinburgh); *Straight Line Crazy* (The Shed, New York/The Bridge Theatre); *The Enormous Crocodile*, *Once on This Island* (Regents Park); *The Glow*, *seven methods of killing kylie jenner* (Public Theatre, New York/ Wooly Mammoth, Washington DC); *Living Newspaper Edition 7, Pah-La* (Royal Court); *The Mirror and the Light* (Gielgud Theatre); *Anna X* (Lowry/Howard Pinter); *Marys Seacole, Blindness* (Donmar Warehouse); *Out West* (Lyric Hammersmith); *The Odyssey* (Unicorn Theatre); *Minority Report* (Nottingham Playhouse, Birmingham Rep, Lyric Theatre); *Inside* (Orange Tree); *Dick Whittington* (National Theatre); *Rockets and Blue Lights* (Royal Exchange); *Faces in the Crowd, Mephisto, Dear Elizabeth, The Human Voice* (The Gate); *Equus* (Theatre Royal Stratford East/UK tour); *Armadillo* (The Yard); *Reasons To Stay Alive* (ETT/UK tour); *One* (HOME/ UK tour/International tour); *Forgotten* (Arcola Theatre /Theatre Royal, Plymouth); *Hive City Legacy* (Roundhouse); *Snowflake* (Kiln Theatre/Old Fire Station); *Fairview* (Young Vic); *Cuckoo* (Soho Theatre); *Nine Foot Nine* (The Bunker/Edinburgh Festival Fringe); *Becoming Shades* (VAULT Festival).

Other credits include: *Twice Born* (Scottish Ballet); *HOME* (Rambert2); *Guardians of the Galaxy: The Live Immersive Experience* (Secret Cinema); *Winter Light* (commissioned by the Museum of the Home); V&A Divas Exhibition.

Her awards include an Olivier Award and WhatsOnStage Award for Best Lighting Design for *My Neighbour Totoro* and a Knight of Illumination Award for Plays and Off West End Award for Best Lighting Design for *Equus*.

XANA | Sound Designer & Composer

XANA is a composer, sound artist, music supervisor and a sound designer developing accessible audio systems for theatre and live art spaces. Xana is the music science and technology lead and project mentor supporting Black artists and inventors at audio research label Inventing Waves. Xana has won the 2023 and 2024 Black British Theatre Award for Best Sound Design.

Theatre credits: *Pig Heart Boy* (Unicorn Theatre); *Shifters* – Offie Finalist, *Barcelona* (Duke of York's Theatre); *The Real Ones, My Father's Fable, Elephant, Sleepova* – Offie Nom, *The P Word* – Offie Nom, *Strange Fruit* (Bush Theatre); *Dead Girls Rising* (Silent Uproar, UK tour), *The Architect* (ATC/GDIF); *Beautiful Thing* (Stratford East); *Imposter 22, Word-Play, Living Newspaper #4* (Royal Court); *Rumble In the Jungle* (Rematch:Live); *Anna Karerina* (Edinburgh Lyceum, Bristol Old Vic); *Intimate Apparel, The Trials, Marys Seacole* (Donmar Warehouse); *Earthworks, Sundown Kiki: Reloaded, The Collaboration, Sundown Kiki, Changing Destiny, Fairview, Ivan and the Dogs* (Young Vic); *...cake* (Theatre Peckham); *Who Killed My Father* (Tron); *as british as a watermelon* (Contact); *Hyde and Seek* (Guildhall); *Burgerz* (Hackney Showroom); *King Troll* (The

Fawn) (Offie Finalist), *Everyday (Deafinitely)* (New Diorama), *Black Holes* (The Place); *Hive City Legacy* (Roundhouse); *Main Character Energy*, *But Daddy I love her*, *Glamrou: From Quran to Queen*, *Curious*, *Half-Breed* (Soho Theatre); *Blood Knot* – Offie Finalist, *Guards At The Taj* – Offie Finalist (Orange Tree Theatre); *Samuel Takes A Break*, *SEX SEX MEN MEN* (Yard Theatre), *Limp Wrist & The Iron Fist*, *Everything I own*, *Is Dat Yu Yeah* (Brixton House).

Theophilus O. Bailey | Movement Director

Theophilus O. Bailey is a multidisciplinary artist based in London, deeply rooted in the fusion of hip-hop and contemporary dance. His work delves into themes of mental health, societal inequities, self-perception, and physical wellness through various mediums, including theatrical performances, filmmaking, and photography.

Over the years, he has collaborated on numerous acclaimed projects, created his own works, produced events, and performed with Olivier Award-winning Hip Hop theatre choreographers Kenrick Sandy and Ivan Blackstock. He has also worked alongside industry-leading choreographers and directors such as Russell Maliphant, Joseph Toonga, Milli Bhatia, and Ryan Calais Cameron.

In the realm of visual art and poetry, Theophilus has choreographed and performed for artists like Julianknxx, Yomi Sode, Caleb Femi, and Rhael 'LionHeart' Cape Hon FRIBA. His recent film work includes appearances in Steven Soderbergh's *Magic Mike's Last Dance* and BSL Zone's *Here/Not Here*.

Bret Yount | Fight Director

Theatre/Opera credits include: *Festen* (Royal Opera House); *Oliver!* (Gielgud); *Twelfth Night* (Royal Shakespeare Company); *King Lear* (The Shed, NYC); *Dr Strangelove* (Noel Coward); *Quiet Songs* (Pit, Barbican); *1984* (Theatre Royal, Bath); *The Spy Who Came in From the Cold* (Chichester Festival Theatre); *Abigail's Party* (Theatre Royal Stratford East); *Carmen* (Glyndebourne); *Machinal* (Old Vic); *The Hungry Body* (Donmar Warehouse); *King Lear* (Wyndhams); *The Witches* (National Theatre); *Cruel Intentions* (The Other Palace); *The Hunt* (St Anns Warehouse, NYC); *My Beautiful Laundrette* (Leicester Curve); *Sleuth*, *Closure* (Theatre Royal, Windsor); *Shooting Hedda Gabler* (Rose Theatre, Kingston); *Macbeth* (Shakespeare's Globe); *The Crucible* (National Theatre/Gielgud); *Mates In Chelsea*, *Hope Has a Happy Meal*, *Imposter 22* (Royal Court); *Village Idiots* (Nottingham Playhouse/Stratford East); *The Harmony Test*, *Between Riverside and Crazy*, *Akedah* (Hampstead Theatre); *The Birthday Party*, *The Deep Blue Sea*, *A View From the Bridge* (West End); *Who's Afraid of Virginia Woolf* (Theatre Royal, Bath);

Dirty Dancing (Dominion Theatre/National Tour); *A Beautiful Thing* (Theatre Royal Stratford East); *Itch* (Opera Holland Park); *A Little Life* (Harold Pinter).

Arthur Carrington | Casting Director

As Casting Director, theatre credits include: *The Glass Menagerie* (Yard); *A Good House, BRACE BRACE, Giant, ECHO, Bluets, Blue Mist, Hope has a Happy Meal, Graceland, Jews. In Their Own Words, A Fight Against..., Maryland, Poet in da Corner* (Royal Court); *King Troll (The Fawn)* (New Diorama); *Paradise Lost (lies unopened beside me)* (Tour); *Little Deaths* (Summerhall); *Visit from an Unknown Woman* (Hampstead); *Liberation Squares* (Nottingham Playhouse/Brixton House & tour); *The Contingency Plan* (Sheffield Crucible); *Barefoot in the Park* (Pitlochry Festival Theatre/Royal Lyceum); *Returning to Haifa* (Finborough); *The Ugly One* (Park); *The Mountaintop* (Young Vic).

As Casting Associate, theatre credits include: *Unicorn* (Garrick); *Dr Strangelove* (Noel Coward); *Waiting for Godot* (Theatre Royal Haymarket); *Slave Play* (Noel Coward); *The Hills of California* (Harold Pinter); *Macbeth* (UK/US Tour); *Lyonesse* (Harold Pinter); *La Cage Aux Folles* (Regents Park Open Air); *The Pillowman* (Duke of York's); *Hamnet* (RSC & Garrick); *Drive Your Plow Over the Bones of the Dead* (Complicité - UK & European tour); *Jerusalem* (Apollo); *Leopoldstadt* (Wyndham's); *Uncle Vanya* (Harold Pinter); *The Night of the Iguana* (Noel Coward); *Rosmersholm* (Duke of York's); *True West* (Vaudeville); *The Ferryman* (Royal Court/Gielgud/Bernard B. Jacobs, New York); *Shipwreck, Albion* (Almeida); *A Very, Very, Very Dark Matter* (Bridge); *Hangmen* (Royal Court/Wyndham's/Atlantic Theatre Company, New York).

Film credits include: *The Unlikely Pilgrimage of Harold Fry; Maryland; Ballywalter.*

Beth Qualter Buncall | Costume Supervisor

Beth Qualter Buncall works as a costume supervisor and maker for film, TV and theatre as well as being a textile artist creating custom and bespoke items such as garments, drapes and sculptural works.

Theatre credits include: *Canned Goods* (Southwark Playhouse); *Goldie Frocks and the Bear Mitzvah* (JW3); *Huddle, The Wolf, The Duck and The Mouse* (Unicorn); *Kim's Convenience* (Riverside Studios/The Park); *The War of the Worlds* (Wilton's Music Hall); *Some Demon* (Arcola Theatre/Bristol Old Vic, Offie nominated); *23.5 Hours, Love Bomb* (National Youth Theatre); *When you pass over my tomb* (Arcola); *The Hatchling* (Wakefield Festival Theatre Co).

Film credits include: *Hostages*; *Greatest Days*; *London's Forgotten*; *Nostalgia Ranch*.

Television credits include: *Mr Loverman*; *A Thousand Blows*; *Trigger Point*; *Top Boy* (BAFTA Winner); *The Witcher*; *The Great*; *The Enfield Poltergeist* (BAFTA Nominated); *The Rings of Power*; *Bridgerton* (CDG Award Nominated); *Ten Percent*; *Call the Midwife*; *Lockwood & Co* (National Film Awards UK Nominated) ; Nike Commercial; LTA Commercial; Bershka Commercial.

Stephen Settle | Associate Lighting Designer & Programmer

Stephen is a freelance Lighting Programmer and Associate based in the UK. He was previously the Lighting Programmer at the Royal Court Theatre where he worked on over 50 productions.

Recent programming credits include: *Retrograde* (Apollo); *The Capulets and the Montagues* (ETO); *The Lonely Londoners* (Kiln); *Robin Hood and the Christmas Heist* (Rose Theatre, Kingston); *The Unseen* (Riverside Studios); *The Turn of the Screw* (Queen's Theatre); *Never Let Me Go* (UK Tour); *A Face in the Crowd* (Young Vic); *Fangirls* (Lyric Hammersmith); *The Secret Garden* (Regents Park); *Beegu*, *The Odyssey* (Unicorn Theatre); *Midsummer [a play with songs]*, *Importance of Being Earnest* (Mercury Theatre); *Macbeth* (UK Tour); *Cinderella* (Churchill Theatre); *Cinderella* (Brixton House); *Backstairs Billy* (Duke of York's); *Hamnet* (Garrick); *Beautiful Thing* (Stratford East).

Wabriya King | Production Dramatherapy

Wabriya King is the Associate Dramatherapist at the Bush Theatre. Wabriya's practice is to create a space and a format to hold people safely while they navigate their experiences in relation to the theatre's work. Wabriya has previously worked on productions at Soho Theatre, Theatre Royal Stratford East, Hampstead Theatre, Royal Court, National Theatre and Paines Plough.

Credits for the Bush include: *Lavender, Hyacinth, Violet, Yew*; *My Father's Fable*; *Shifters* (also West End); *Paradise Now!*; *The P Word*; *House of Ife*; *Red Pitch*; *Overflow*; *Lava*; *The High Table*.

Adam Jefferys | Production Manager

Adam Jefferys is a Lighting Designer and Production Manager from Essex. Previously, he was the Technical Manager of the New Diorama Theatre.

Recent Work: *The Bleeding Tree*, *Under The Kundè Tree* (Southwark

Playhouse); *The Great Privation* (Theatre503); *The Olive Boy* (UK tour); *Murder In The Dark* (UK tour); *Communion, The End, My Father's Fable, Elephant* (Bush); *It Is I, Seagull* (UK tour); *Soon, Pilot* (Summerhall); *Philosophy of The World* (Cambridge Junction); *After The Act, War & Culture* (New Diorama); *Project Dictator* (New Diorama/Edinburgh); *Jekyll and Hyde* (Derby Playhouse); *Everything Has Changed* (Tour/Edinburgh); *Dorian* (Reading Rep).

For more of Adam's work please visit his website: adamjefferys.com

Stacey Nurse | Company Stage Manager

Stacey Nurse is a multifaceted Theatre Technician, Lighting Designer and Stage Manager who loves being able to see a creative process through from initial conception to final production.

Theatre credits include: *The Lonely Londoners (*Assistant Stage Manager/Book Cover: Kiln Theatre); *The Glorious French Revolution, King Troll (The Fawn)* (Company Stage Manager: New Diorama); *G* (Deputy Stage Manager: Royal Court); *Between The Lines (*Company Stage Manager: New Diorama), *For Black Boys Who Have Considered Suicide When The Hue Gets Too Heavy* (Assistant Stage Manager: New Diorama, Royal Court, Apollo Theatre Shaftsbury); *To Hold My Love (*Lighting Designer: The Place, Resolution Festival); *Summer Camp For Broken People (*Stage Manager and Lighting Designer: Pleasance London and Edinburgh Fringe); *Blueprints* (Stage Manager and Lighting Designer: Pleasance London and Edinburgh Fringe); *I Love You Now What (*Stage Manager: Edinburgh Fringe); *Brenda's Got A Baby (*Stage Manager: New Diorama).

Alexander Standish-Murray | Assistant Stage Manager

Alexander Standish-Murray recently graduated from the University of East London where he studied Performing Arts and specialised in experimental, ritualistic, divisive theatre.

He is a passionate early career Stage Manager who has already worked on multiple professional theatre productions, such as (Rehearsal) Stage Manager on *The Glorious French Revolution* and Stage Manager for Win(d)ing Orchestra's *R&D3*.

Alex is also a dedicated theatre technician, being involved in many productions as an operator, displaying his skill in understanding the technical aspects that bring a show together.

Titilola Dawudu | Dramaturg

Titilola Dawudu is the Associate Dramaturg at the Bush Theatre, heading up the Literary department. She works with the Artistic Director and Associate Artistic Director to commission and nurture news plays and ideas, working closely with writers, managing writing groups and the talent development pipeline.

Titilola was the dramaturg for an early iteration at Ovalhouse of Tyrell Williams's award-winning play *Red Pitch*. She dramaturgically supported some of the RSC's 37 Plays winners, most notably *Dreaming and Drowning* by Kwame Owusu.

Titilola co-created and edited *Hear Me Now Audition Monologues for Actors of Colour* with Tamasha Theatre Company, published by Oberon Books. *Hear Me Now Volume Two* was published in August 2022 by Methuen Drama. As a writer, Titilola has written for Theatre Royal Arojah in Abuja, Nigeria, Theatre Peckham, Ovalhouse, Beyond Face and Soho Theatre.

Bush Theatre

We make theatre for London. Now.

For over 50 years the Bush Theatre has been a world-famous home for new plays and an internationally renowned champion of playwrights.

Combining ambitious artistic programming with meaningful community engagement work and industry leading talent development schemes, the Bush Theatre champions and supports unheard voices to develop the artists and audiences of the future.

Since opening in 1972 the Bush has produced more than 500 ground-breaking premieres of new plays, developing an enviable reputation for its acclaimed productions nationally and internationally.

They have nurtured the careers of writers including James Graham, Lucy Kirkwood, Temi Wilkey, Jonathan Harvey and Jack Thorne. Recent successes include Tyrell Williams' **Red Pitch**, Benedict Lombe's **Shifters**, and Arinzé Kene's **Misty**. The Bush has won over 100 awards including the Olivier Award for Outstanding Achievement in Affiliate Theatre for the past four years for Richard Gadd's **Baby Reindeer**, Igor Memic's **Old Bridge**, Waleed Akhtar's **The P Word** and Matilda Feyişayọ Ibini's **Sleepova**.

Located in the renovated old library on Uxbridge Road in the heart of Shepherd's Bush, the Bush Theatre continues to create a space where all communities can be part of its future and call the theatre home.

> **'The place to go for ground-breaking work as diverse as its audiences'** Evening Standard

bushtheatre.co.uk
@bushtheatre

Artistic Director	Lynette Linton
Executive Director	Mimi Findlay
Associate Director	Katie Greenall
Deputy Executive Director	Angela Wachner
Development & Marketing Assistant	Nicima Abdi
Head of Marketing	Shannon Clarke
Head of Development	Jocelyn Cox
Associate Dramaturg	Titilola Dawudu
Finance Assistant	Lauren Francis
Technical & Buildings Manager	Jamie Haigh
Freelance Producer	Emma Halstead
Assistant Venue Manager	Rae Harm
Head of Finance	Neil Harris
Marketing Officer	Laela Henley-Rowe
Lead Producer	Nikita Karia
Community Producing Assistant	Joanne Leung
Event Sales Manager	Simon Pilling
Senior Technician	John Pullig
Production Technician	Charlie Sadler
Venue Manager (Theatre)	Ade Seriki
Press Manager	Martin Shippen
Community Producer	Holly Smith
Marketing Manager	Ed Theakston
Marketing Officer	Kelly Thurston
Assistant Venue Manager (Box Office)	Robin Wilks
Theatre Administrator	Pauline Walker
Café Bar Manager	Wayne Wilson

DUTY MANAGERS
Sara Dawood, Molly Elson, Thomas Ingram, Madeleine Simpson-Kent & Anna-May Wood.

VENUE SUPERVISORS
Antony Baker, Addy Caulder-James, Emma Chatel, Zea Hilland, Nzuzi Malemda, Roy Mas, Jacob Meier & Louis Nicholson.

VENUE ASSISTANTS
Javine Aduganfi, Doridan Bavangila, Manuel Ruiz, Will Byam-Shaw, Pyerre Clarke, Daniel Fesoom, Matias Hailu, Bo Leandro, Maya Li Preti, Ishani McGuire, Khy Matinez, Ed Mendoza, Carys Murray, Chana Nardone, James Robertson, Ali Shah & Nefertari Williams.

BOARD OF TRUSTEES
Uzma Hasan (Chair), Mark Dakin, Kim Evans, Keerthi Kollimada, Lynette Linton, Anthony Marraccino, Jim Marshall, Rajiv Nathwani, Kwame Owusu, Stephen Pidcock & Catherine Score.

THANK YOU

Our supporters make our work possible Together, we're evolving the canon and creating a bolder, more diverse, and representative future for British theatre We're so grateful to you all.

MAJOR DONORS
Charles Holloway OBE
Jim & Michelle Gibson
Georgia Oetker
Cathy & Tim Score
Susie Simkins
Jack Thorne
Gianni & Michael Alen-Buckley

SHOOTING STARS
Jim & Michelle Gibson
Anthony Marraccino & Mariela Manso
Cathy & Tim Score
Susie Simkins

LONE STARS
Clyde Cooper
Adam Kenwright
Jim Marshall
Georgia Oetker

HANDFUL OF STARS
Charlie Bigham
Judy Bollinger
Richard & Sarah Clarke
Christopher delaMare
David des Jardins
Sue Fletcher
Thea Guest
Kate Hamer Ltd
Elizabeth Jack
Simon & Katherine Johnson
Joanna Kennedy
Garry & Lorna Lawrence
Phyllida Lloyd & Kate Pakenham
Vivienne Lukey
Sam & Jim Murgatroyd

Mark & Anne Paterson
Nick & Annie Reid
Bhagat Sharma
Dame Emma Thompson
Joe Tinston & Amelia Knott

RISING STARS
Elizabeth Beebe
Matthew Cushen
Anne-Hélène and Rafaël Biosse Duplan
Martin Blackburn
David Brooks
Catharine Browne
Anthony Chantry
Lauren Clancy
Caroline Clasen
Susan Cuff
Austin Erwin
Kim Evans
Mimi Findlay
Jack Gordon
Hugh & Sarah Grootenhuis
Sarah Harrison
Uzma Hasan
Lesley Hill & Russ Shaw
Davina & Malcolm Judelson
Mike Lewis
Lynette Linton
Tim & Deborah Maunder
Michael McCoy
Judy Mellor
Caro Millington
Rajiv Nathwani
Yoana Nenova
Stephen Pidcock
Miguel & Valeri Ramos Handal
James St. Ville KC

Jan Topham Kit & Anthony va Tulleken

CORPORATE SPONSORS
Biznography
Casting Pictures Ltd.
Nick Hern Books
S&P Global
The Agency

TRUSTS & FOUNDATIONS
Backstage Trust
Buffini Chao Foundation
Christina Smith Foundation
Daisy Trust
Esmée Fairbairn Foundation
Garrick Charitable Trust
Hammersmith United Charities
The Golsoncott Foundation
The Headley Trust
Idlewild Trust
Jerwood Foundation
John Lyon's Charity
Martin Bowley Charitable Trust
Noël Coward Foundation
Royal Victoria Hall Foundation
The Thistle Trust

And all the donors who wish to remain anonymous.

If you are interested in finding out how to be involved, please visit **bushtheatre.co.uk/support-us** email **development@bushtheatre.co.uk** or call **020 8743 3584**.

SPEED

Mohamed-Zain Dada

Acknowledgements

Thanks to Arian Nik, Nikesh Patel, Shazia Nicholls, Sabrina Sandhu, Rachel Taylor and particularly Milli Bhatia.

Thanks to the company: Tomás Palmer, Stacey Nurse, Alex Standish-Murray, Theophilus O. Bailey, XANA, Beth Qualter Buncall, Jessica Hung Han Yun, Arthur Carrington and Bret Yount. And to Titilola Dawudu, Lynette Linton, Daniel Bailey and everyone at the Bush Theatre.

Thanks to my parents, Fehmida and Ashraf Dada, and my siblings: Zara Al Akku, Nadia Dada, Humzah Al Akku and Nadir Dada.

Thanks to Will-Nyerere Plastow for being a constant source of inspiration as a human being by demonstrating what solidarity in action looks like.

Special thanks to Gurnesha Bola for your encouragement and unconditional support.

M-Z.D.

Characters

ABZ, *thirty-eight, the lead facilitator*
SAMIR, *twenty-seven, a delivery driver*
HARLEEN, *twenty-eight, a nurse*
FAIZA, *thirty-four, an entrepreneur*

Note

The play oscillates between the Speed Awareness and Aggressive Driving course in a hotel basement and a dissociative space that only Abz experiences called the 'Johari Window'. In the 'Johari Window', time is suspended and Abz is caught up in a moment of past trauma without the participants of the course noticing, though they might be activated within it.

As the play progresses, the 'Johari Window' becomes more prominent, as a memory getting closer and closer. Abz is desperately trying to suppress the memory. The 'memories' are of a high-speed chase that ends in a crash – each one feels more dangerous than the last.

This text went to press before the end of rehearsals and so may differ slightly from the play as performed.

ACT ONE

Prologue

A conference room, ABZ picks up a bouquet of flowers. A low hum and a brief flicker as ABZ enters the Johari Window for a moment. He finds himself back in the present.

Scene One

The conference room – in the basement of a nondescript budget hotel. SAMIR, FAIZA *and* HARLEEN *are seated and facing* ABZ.

ABZ *has a small table in front of him, a 'Keep Calm and Carry On' mug. Next to him there is a flip-chart with markers, and a TV cart.*

There is a fish tank fixed into the wall with three goldfish in it, a watercolour painting of a fruit bowl by Winston Churchill, and one poster that says: REBUILD YOUR RESPONSIBILITY. ABZ *is putting up another poster: WITHOUT RULES, WE ARE NOTHING BUT ANIMALS – SOCRATES.*

On the other side of the room is a cramped break-room area with a vending machine, a cheap-looking sofa and a shaft with a small kitchenette.

ABZ	Right, it's just a small group so let's get into some quick intros. Hello everyone, I'm Abz.
SAMIR	What's that short for?
ABZ	Let's start here.

ABZ *points at* FAIZA.

FAIZA	I'm Faiza Awan.
ABZ	– First name only, please.
FAIZA	And I'm the CEO of Asia Specific. One of the biggest modest fashion brands in the UK –
ABZ	No other personal information is necessary. Where are you from, Faiza?
FAIZA	I live in St Albans.
ABZ	Thank you. Would you like to go next?
	ABZ *points at* HARLEEN.
HARLEEN	I'm Harleen, from Birmingham.
SAMIR	(*To* HARLEEN.) Brummie, yeah?
ABZ	Last but not least.
SAMIR	Samir.
ABZ	And where are you from, Samir?
SAMIR	West Yorkshire.
ABZ	Where in West Yorkshire?
SAMIR	H-town.
ABZ	H-town?
SAMIR	Harehills, Leeds.
	Are those piranhas in the fish tank?
HARLEEN	(*To* SAMIR.) Goldfish.
ABZ	Thank you all.
	ABZ *paces around the conference room.*
	Driving is not a human right, it's a privilege. You've got to earn it. Why? Because twenty-five thousand people are injured a year. Life-altering injuries.

ACT ONE, SCENE ONE   7

SAMIR   My chacha, Talal, injured his foot in a car crash once.

(*Serious*.) Never drive in bata chappal.

ABZ   Five people die every day because of road traffic deaths. Children, adults, your pet dog. The road does not discriminate.

I spent three years working with The Royal Society for the Prevention of Accidents. RoSPA.

Young lads on laughing gas weaving between traffic, four-by-fours tailgating and flashing like no man's business. Red lights meaning nothing now. Amber even less. England is falling apart.

Silence.

Everyone selected here has been served fines for a combination of 'speeding' and 'aggressive driving'.

FAIZA   It's ironic because I'm the least aggressive person you'll ever meet.

ABZ   I'd like you all to turn to each other. Go on. Turn to each other. What do you see?

SAMIR   Um.

ABZ pauses for a moment.

ABZ   – You're all mirrors. That's right. Mirrors. Reflections of each other. You see each other but what you really see, is yourself. Warts and all.

ABZ refers to his clipboard.

I can see from my notes that you're all on nine points. If you were to take the points instead of participating, we'd be revoking or suspending your licence.

SAMIR	Nah, like a ban?
ABZ	Yes.
HARLEEN	The letter I received mentioned 'on-road altercations'?
ABZ	Right, thank you, Helene. On-road altercations is the inevitable result of aggressive driving. Defined as operating a vehicle in a manner that endangers people or property.
SAMIR	Why property?
ABZ	*Too Fast, Too Furious* has never felt so apt.
SAMIR	Heavy film.
HARLEEN	I think they might have exaggerated what I've done.
SAMIR	Yeah, same.
ABZ	The police reports would suggest otherwise.
FAIZA	I'd dispute anything you *think* you've read about me.
ABZ	Do you want the good news?
FAIZA	Please.
ABZ	You could be in a magistrates' court. You could be sat at home, without your licence. You could have been fined.
	But instead, you're here.
	You're probably thinking 'how' and 'why'. Who gave me this second chance? But this isn't the your run-of-the-mill speed awareness course. The stick doesn't always work, sometimes you need a bit of carrot. I'm glad the DVLA recognise that.

ACT ONE, SCENE ONE

	You're here today as part of a new scheme the DVLA are trialling, designed to help road users who are repeat offenders when it comes to speeding and aggressive driving. And I'm delighted to say that you three are the first to take part.
HARLEEN	What do we need to do to 'pass'?
ABZ	Radical listening and meaningful engagement, Helene.
	And of course, the DVLA will be evaluating your progress for six months after the completion of your course.
HARLEEN	It's Har-leen. What do you mean by 'evaluating'? And are all the other participants Asian?
SAMIR	Woah, Abinav, that's a good point, you know.
FAIZA	I wouldn't be surprised. Probably all young Asian lads. I've seen too much on the M6.
SAMIR	Abishek, is it all aapneh?
	ABZ *grabs the TV cart and wheels it over to the centre.*
ABZ	Okay. Can we stop the side-bar conversations, please. This short video will clarify everything.
	He turns on the TV and starts the video. On the TV screen, ABZ *appears, walking toward the camera on a quiet side street.*
	(*On the TV.*) Welcome to the Driving and Licensing Agency's new pilot scheme: Rehabilitating and Unlearning. The National Driving Initiative. R.U.N.D.I.

	(*To the group*.) That's me.
	(*On the TV*.) You have probably attended one of the National Speed Awareness Courses either online or in-person because you have exceeded the speed limit in a zone where the speeding restrictions have been clearly marked.
	This is usually a two hour and forty-five-minute course. R.U.N.D.I. is an all-day course.
SAMIR	(*To* HARLEEN.) These lot need to change the name.
ABZ	Focus please.
	The video cuts to ABZ *standing behind a car boot.*
	(*On the TV*.) So what is R.U.N.D.I.?
	SAMIR *tries to stop himself from laughing*.
FAIZA	What's so funny?
HARLEEN	(*To* SAMIR.) Hold it together.
ABZ	(*On the* TV.) It's a brand-new pilot scheme being trialled by the DVLA to rehabilitate aggressive drivers.
	ABZ *is sat in a car, revving an engine*.
	(*On the TV*.) We know as much as you do, that there is probably a lot more bubbling away under the surface when you're driving. From issues at home to problems with your boss. Life can be hard.
	ABZ *opens the bonnet of the car. He sniffs the engine*.
	Can you smell that engine oil? We want to get inside of you and find out what the

problem is. So after we're done, you can keep calm and drive safe.

ABZ *squatting near a tyre holding a wrench.*

You're probably wondering who I am? I'm Abz. And I'm a speed-awareness facilitator and an anger management specialist.

So welcome to R.U.N.D.I. You're lucky enough to be one of the one hundred participants to trial this scheme.

Get ready for your personal driving MOT. Let's go!

An image of the R.U.N.D.I. *logo.*

The data we take for the scheme will be used to decide whether a national roll-out occurs or not. Refusal to comply with the DVLA will result in three points on your licence. The DVLA is not legally responsible for the breach or leak or sale of your data to third party subsidiaries.

The video ends. ABZ *turns the TV off and wheels the TV cart away.*

ABZ   Any questions?

FAIZA *raises her hand.*

Yes.

FAIZA   More of a comment than a question: I'm really relieved we've got the opportunity to prove ourselves.

ABZ   That's the spirit, Faiza.

HARLEEN *rolls her eyes.*

Alright, let's set some ground rules. Firstly, whatever you share in this room, stays in this room. What happens in Vegas, stays in Vegas. And don't worry if you get it wrong, we're all here to learn.

Secondly, no verbal or physical abuse. Avoid any F-bombs, C-bombs or D-bombs. Any bomb really.

Thirdly, there is strictly no phone usage allowed while the course is running.

You'll be receiving some feedback forms at the end.

ABZ hands out feedback forms to SAMIR, FAIZA and HARLEEN.

Right. Let's start by reminding ourselves on the basics of speeding.

ABZ picks up Road Rules: The Ultimate Guide to Driving *from the table.*

This book is my bible.

SAMIR   That's straight bid'ah.

ABZ   The *Road Rules* guide has everything you'll need. You need to know what the speed limit is where there are no signs. This will tell you. You want to refresh yourself on the specifics of creeping out at a T-junction, this is for you.

Right. Shall we have a little quiz?

SAMIR   (*To* HARLEEN.) I'm applying to be on *Tipping Point*.

ABZ   Let's get started. Turn over your evaluation sheet forms.

ABZ grabs a stack of papers from his desk, he hands SAMIR, FAIZA and HARLEEN some pencils.

Everyone ready?

HARLEEN	Yep.
FAIZA	Born ready.
ABZ	Number one, what does the anagram PHEV stand for.
HARLEEN	I think it's an acronym.
ABZ	Quiet please.
	PHEV. P-HEV or PA-HEV. Depending on how you want to say it.
SAMIR	(*To* HARLEEN.) My man Abdullah is about to spit some bars.
ABZ	Is it:
	A: Peugeot Hatchback Electric Vehicle.
	B: Pass here, easy vantage.
	Or C: A plug-in hybrid electric vehicle.
	Everyone got that? Number two. In icy conditions, how much does breaking distance need to increase by?
	A: Three times.
	B: Ten times.
	Or C: Twenty times.
	Finally, number three. A pedestrian hit by a car travelling at thirty mph has a one in five chance of being killed. What are the chances at thirty-five mph?
FAIZA	I hit a pheasant once on a country road, accidentally.
	Feathers bloody everywhere.
ABZ	Is it:
	A: One in three.

	B: One in four.
	Or C: no difference.
	Everyone hear that? Yeah. I am seeing nods.
HARLEEN	Hold on. Done.
FAIZA	Nailed that.
ABZ	Correct answers were... drum roll please.
	For question one. It was... C. PHEV is a plug-in-hybrid electric vehicle.
SAMIR	EVs got proper fast acceleration.
ABZ	Samir, please. Number two. The answer is... B. The breaking distance for icy roads is ten times.
	And finally... are we ready?
	You've got a one in three chance of killing a pedestrian at thirty-five mph.
FAIZA	Yes! Mr Abz, that was B right?
ABZ	No, that was A.
FAIZA	Oh fudge.
ABZ	Show of hands, who got three out of three?
	ABZ *scans the room. No one raises their hands.*
	Two out of three?
	No one raises their hands.
	One out of three?
	FAIZA *proudly raises her hand.* SAMIR *nonchalantly raises his hand.* FAIZA *reaches over to see* SAMIR*'s worksheet.*
FAIZA	Get in!

ACT ONE, SCENE ONE 15

ABZ	(*To* HARLEEN.) I'm assuming you got zero out of three.
HARLEEN	I thought I'd get at least one.
SAMIR	(*To* HARLEEN.) I've never been good at these either.
FAIZA	Do the winners get anything? Like all my points wiped off our licences?
ABZ	No. And clearly, you all need to do your theory tests again.

He grabs the flip-chart paper and reveals the national speed limit sign.

When you see this sign, what's the speed limit?

Pop your hand up if you know the answer.

HARLEEN	The national limit or something –

ABZ *silently puts his hand up to remind* HARLEEN. *She puts her hand up.*

ABZ	Yes?
HARLEEN	It's the national speed limit?
ABZ	And what's the national speed limit –
	– on a single carriageway?
HARLEEN	Okay, um, seventy mph.
ABZ	Wrong. Faiza?
FAIZA	Is it ninety mph?
ABZ	That's worrying, Faiza.
SAMIR	Oh Abijit. I know this one, it's one-hundred mph. That's the sign for the autobahn motorway out in Germany. Me and my boys planned a road trip out there.

ABZ	A car's speedometer can be a killer's gauge and you would all be serial killers. It's sixty mph.
	ABZ flips the paper over and reveals a STOP sign.
	What's this?
	ABZ paces the room. He puts his hand on SAMIR's shoulder.
	What is that? Any ideas?
SAMIR	Brother, eurgh.
	(*To* HARLEEN.) His breath smells like crisps.
	HARLEEN puts her hand up.
HARLEEN	It's a STOP sign.
FAIZA	I was *about* to say that.
ABZ	Exactly.
	ABZ hastily turns over the flipchart paper and draws a Give Way sign.
	Anyone know what this is?
	HARLEEN puts her hand up.
HARLEEN	Giving way.
ABZ	Almost. It's a Give Way sign.
HARLEEN	(*Under her breath.*) That's what I said.
ABZ	How about this, why don't we do what these two signs are telling us?
SAMIR	Right now.
ABZ	Right this second. Let's stop and let's give way… to our feelings.
	The group groan.

ACT ONE, SCENE ONE

We ready to get into it?

ABZ grabs a pen and a clipboard and stares at them for a moment.

HARLEEN — Are we meant to do something or –

ABZ — – You tell me?

HARLEEN — What do you mean?

FAIZA — Is this a test?

ABZ — Rehabilitation starts with looking at ourselves with honesty.

Self-reflection. Why are you here?

ABZ writes 'Why are you here?' on the flip chart and gets into a squat position.

Silence.

This is a no-judgement zone.

FAIZA tentatively puts her hand up.

Go ahead.

FAIZA — I think I'm here because I'm misunderstood.

ABZ — Go on.

FAIZA — I don't get angry, people get angry at me. In fact, I've only ever sworn once in a car... in English.

SAMIR — What was the swear word?

ABZ — Not relevant, Samir.

FAIZA — The C-word.

ABZ — Okay, Faiza, what made you swear –

FAIZA — Cunt, obviously.

ABZ — Let's stick to the rules I set out, okay. Can we all do that?

FAIZA	Everyone says it, don't they?
ABZ	It might be worth considering why everyone gets angry at you, Faiza.
	Samir?
SAMIR	Abzy, I'll be real, I'm a pretty zen guy.
ABZ	That doesn't answer my question.
SAMIR	What was the question?
ABZ	Why are you here?
SAMIR	On this course?
ABZ	You've got nine points on your licence. Why are you here?
SAMIR	I don't always drive fast but I'd been known to take shilijat.
FAIZA	Driving under the influence.
SAMIR	It's like a herb.
ABZ	Shilajit?
SAMIR	You know what it was. They say you shouldn't take it if you're married. I'm not. But I bought it anyway. It's like taking in NOS in *Need for Speed* except for humans.
ABZ	You know what I think, maybe it's not the herb, but your own behaviour.
SAMIR	What?
ABZ	(*To* HARLEEN.) And you?
HARLEEN	I gave someone a gentle reminder.
ABZ	About?
HARLEEN	Their behaviour.
ABZ	What was the reminder?
HARLEEN	It was a back and forth in a car park.

ABZ	That's all it was?
HARLEEN	I'm hardly Ronnie Pickering, okay.
SAMIR	That man is a living legend.
ABZ	Alright, let's park that for now.
	You're probably wondering why I asked you to self-reflect. Being angry puts you in a state of adrenaline and your cortisol rises.
	Your emotions are clouded and you're putting ordinary British people in danger. I'm going to need you to be honest with yourselves and each other to get to those triggers today.

ABZ jots something down on the clipboard and then turns the flip chart to reveal the JOHARI WINDOW – a table with four quadrants. On the top left corner it says 'ARENA', on the bottom left it says 'MASK', on the top right it says 'BLIND SPOT' and the bottom right says 'UNCONSCIOUS'.

ABZ	Anyone know what this is? No?
	It's the Johari Window.
SAMIR	The Jihadi window?
ABZ	JOHARI. JO-HARI.
SAMIR	*(To himself.)* JO-HARI.
HARLEEN	*(Under her breath.)* He can pronounce that but not Harleen?
ABZ	It was designed to help us understand ourselves better. Because self-awareness is self-control.

ABZ points at the flip chart.

The arena is what everyone sees, including yourself. Your brand.

FAIZA | So important.

ABZ | Your unknowns are your hidden feelings that no one knows.

Not even yourself. It comes out unexpectedly, like gas.

Your blindspot is what other people can see, but you can't.

Your mask is what you choose to hide.

The Johari Window is a portal into your subconscious.

HARLEEN *puts her hand up.*

Today, we're going to look into your unknowns, we're going to expose your blind spots and we're going to get rid of those masks.

By the end of this course, you're going to be transformed as drivers.

ABZ *pauses.*

And as human bei–

A phone starts ringing

– Okay, whose phone is ringing?

SAMIR, FAIZA *and* HARLEEN *look at each other.*

SAMIR | – I think it might be yours.

ABZ *glances at his phone.*

You know what, how about we take five?

FAIZA | Already?

ABZ | Yeah, go ahead. There is a vending machine and kitchen over there.

SAMIR	Sick.
FAIZA	Abz, what's the Wi-Fi?
ABZ	I'm afraid there is none.
FAIZA	I beg your pardon?
HARLEEN	We're in the basement of a Holiday Inn.
SAMIR	Long. My boy Iffy was gonna tell me when to pull out of MagaCoin.
FAIZA	No Wi-Fi at all? Because I haven't got any blooming phone signal either.
ABZ	It's okay, that's why you left an emergency contact with us.
	If anything comes up, I'll be notified.
FAIZA	I manage multiple businesses.
ABZ	Question: are you allowed your phone when you drive?
	Silence.
	Arrive alive, don't text and drive. Off you go.
FAIZA	(*To* HARLEEN *and* SAMIR.) Have either of you got signal?
	SAMIR *and* HARLEEN *check their phone.*
SAMIR	Nah.
FAIZA	Ahem. Mr Abz.
ABZ	Faiza.
FAIZA	I have a request.
ABZ	Please.
FAIZA	Well, as a CEO –
ABZ	– If it's about your Wi-Fi, I really can't help you –

FAIZA	– I'm a key stakeholder so I thought I'd pop outside to check a really important email.
ABZ	It's a short break, I'd appreciate if you don't leave the space at this time.
FAIZA	I don't think you understand the scale of this. It's a potential investment in Asia Specific by an Indonesian venture capital fund, this could make or break my company.
ABZ	I'm afraid the answer is no.
FAIZA	You realise, my absence could have an impact on the economy?
ABZ	We survived Liz Truss, I'm sure we'll be okay.

ABZ's phone rings again. He picks it up.

Hello? HELLO? I can't hear anything. Give us a minute, I'm in the basement.

ABZ exits the basement.

Scene Two

The conference room.

FAIZA	How has he got signal?
SAMIR	He's probably on T-Mobile.

HARLEEN and SAMIR wander over to the break-room area with FAIZA close behind. The three of them sit down.

FAIZA	I think he's gatekeeping the password. The one day I need my phone to function.
SAMIR	(*To* HARLEEN.) What's your story then?

HARLEEN	It's speed awareness, not speed dating.
SAMIR	Oh, no, I'm not trying it. And technically, it's also about aggressive driving, I'm not aggressive though.
HARLEEN	I actually believe that you know.
	SAMIR *smiles to himself.*
	Why you smiling?
SAMIR	Is it a crime to smile?
HARLEEN	No, no. As you were.
FAIZA	God, there is like a *really* musty smell in here.
	SAMIR *walks over to open the kitchenette shutters, to search through the cupboards for a glass before spotting the vending machine.*
HARLEEN	I can't smell anything.
	Silence. They both fake smile at each other. FAIZA *looks at her nails and* HARLEEN *stares at the ceiling.*
FAIZA	So umm, what are you *actually* in for?
HARLEEN	I couldn't even tell you.
	SAMIR *puts some change in the vending machine.*
FAIZA	A 'gentle back and forth' in a car park.
HARLEEN	Don't even remember what it was.
	Silence except for SAMIR *fidgeting with the vending machine.*
FAIZA	Gosh, to think we were that close to losing our licences.
HARLEEN	That was not an option for me.

FAIZA	I know, same. I'd have to take the bloody train everywhere.
HARLEEN	It would have meant waking up two hours earlier to get to work and I'd have to miss night shifts. Let alone taking my Nani to appointments.
FAIZA	What about you?
SAMIR	I only just got a stage two re-map done on my Golf-R. Unreal grip. Fresh wrap, quad pipe trim, twenty-two plate, alloy rims, triple exhaust.

SAMIR *walks over to show them a picture of his car on his phone.*

HARLEEN	Oh lovely.
SAMIR	(*To* HARLEEN.) Bad-boy engine. Wait till you hear me rev it.
	Anyway, there's no way we're gonna get a ban. I've done these before, you just gotta sit through it.
HARLEEN	I get the feeling that Abz won't let us sit through anything.
SAMIR	It's like he's had couple cans of Monster this morning.
HARLEEN	He's got a lot of energy and a lot of mottos.
FAIZA	(*To* SAMIR.) Are you a mechanic then?

SAMIR *walks back over to the vending machine.*

SAMIR	A bit of DPD, a bit of Deliveroo, aspiring entrepreneur.
FAIZA	A real mixed bag.
	(*To* HARLEEN.) What do you do?

HARLEEN	I'm a nurse.
FAIZA	Oh, clap for the carers.
HARLEEN	It's a mess.
FAIZA	I recently went private.
HARLEEN	Okay.
FAIZA	You get bumped forward on *everything*. Appointments, scans.
	Even surgery.
HARLEEN	Sounds like you're doing well then.
FAIZA	Doing well with?
HARLEEN	You mentioned a business.
FAIZA	Oh yes, my brand, Asia Specific –
	– That's why I'm a bit anxious to see if this deal happens.

SAMIR *shakes the vending machine.* FAIZA *and* HARLEEN *turn around to look at him.*

HARLEEN	What kind of stuff do you sell?
FAIZA	Everything you can think of. Think Khaadi but couture, high, high couture.
HARLEEN	So do you do saris and shalwar kameez?
FAIZA	Do you wear *saris?*
HARLEEN	For shaadis and stuff, yeah.
FAIZA	And if it were, hypothetically, a hybrid of a sari and something more modern? Like if Fendi and Ritu Kumar had a love child.
HARLEEN	I guess, if it was affordable.
FAIZA	What price range? Are we talking Primark? H&M?

HARLEEN	Maybe H&M –
	– Are you doing market research on me?
FAIZA	Of course not.
	FAIZA *writes 'H&M and TURKISH SUPPLIERS' on a piece of paper.*
	SAMIR *starts to kick the vending machine.* HARLEEN *looks over.*
HARLEEN	Kicking it won't help.
	SAMIR *comes back.*
SAMIR	I got scammed.
HARLEEN	By who?
SAMIR	The vending machine.
HARLEEN	I don't think an inanimate object can scam you, m'love.
SAMIR	You Punjabi?
FAIZA	Are you chatting her up?
SAMIR	Nah, no.
HARLEEN	Lahore, you?
SAMIR	Mum's side is. Gujranwala, Pakistan.
HARLEEN	West Punjab, then?
SAMIR	Oh you're on that.
HARLEEN	Oh you're on that. Sanjha Punjab you mean? Okay, Mr Nationalist.
SAMIR	(*To* FAIZA.) What about you?
FAIZA	St Albans.
SAMIR	Nah, like, originally? 'Cause you don't look Pakistani.
FAIZA	Oh, thank you.

ACT ONE, SCENE TWO 27

HARLEEN — Are you Pakistani?

FAIZA — I'm Urdu-speaking and half Memon. Although I did do one of those ancestry-dot-com tests and found out I had a great uncle from the Yemen.

SAMIR — Can you speak Arabic then?

FAIZA — Shwaya, shwaya.

SAMIR — Mad. You were on that show right?

FAIZA *looks up*.

FAIZA — I do *a lot* of press.

SAMIR — The business show, shit, I forgot the name.

FAIZA — Do you mean *Dragon's Den*?

SAMIR — Yeah, that whole drinks thing you pitched.

FAIZA — Golden Boost.

SAMIR — So clever. Had that little animated character on the front, like Naruto but sipping like a –

FAIZA — Gold bar –

SAMIR — – Like outta this teet, right?

HARLEEN — A gold bar with a teet?

FAIZA — An early concept idea that we were refining. An animated character seeking sustenance from a cow's udder. Symbolising nutrition.

HARLEEN — What's golden about it?

FAIZA — Turmeric root energy drink. It had huge potential. Global markets in India. We were stocked in Waitrose.

HARLEEN — As in haldi doodh?

SAMIR — That Theo Paphitis guy is a prick.

FAIZA	You're thinking of Touker Suleyman. Theo is a sweetheart.
SAMIR	What about that Huel guy, he seems sound?
FAIZA	Well…
HARLEEN	What? I like Huel.
FAIZA	He's broke.
	ABZ re-enters looking visibly disturbed and staring at the fish tank.
SAMIR	Is it? He's got *The Diary of a CEO*, though?
FAIZA	It's an open secret in the industry.
SAMIR	It's all smokey mirrors.
HARLEEN	How did you get on in *Dragon's Den*?
FAIZA	Deborah Meaden made an offer. But I said no.
HARLEEN	Why?
FAIZA	She wanted thirty per cent equity.
SAMIR	Brave call.
FAIZA	Too big a cut.
SAMIR	You still running it?
FAIZA	Sold it to a Japanese investor.
HARLEEN	Why did you sell?
FAIZA	The FSA don't want brown women to succeed.
SAMIR	FSA?
FAIZA	The Food Standards Agency.
SAMIR	Yeah, that's annoying.
HARLEEN	What did they say?

FAIZA	'Diluting the key ingredient' whatever that means. And 'inaccuracies on the label'. It's all very political, especially with competitors in the market.
	A hum creeps in that only ABZ can hear. ABZ enters the Johari Window and the hum is causing him considerable distress. A light shines and he is blinded by it. Sparks fly and ABZ jumps back. The hum gets louder and louder and louder.
	ABZ returns to the present catches his breath with his hand on his chest.
SAMIR	(*To* FAIZA.) Listen, I got this app idea, it basically tells you where to find the best car mechanics locally and a rating system to tell you who's good and who's ripping you off.
	Could I get your business brain on it?
FAIZA	Let's keep talking.
ABZ	L-l-let's get back to it, eh?
SAMIR	(*To* FAIZA.) Cool, yeah. It's called 'We Fix Any Gaddi' if you wanted the Insta handle.
FAIZA	Not now.

ACT TWO

Scene One

HARLEEN, SAMIR *and* FAIZA *walk back to the conference-room area.* ABZ *is pacing around the room nervously.* ABZ *turns over the flipchart paper and frantically writes 'WHY DO YOU SPEED?'*

ABZ	OKAY.
	Why. Do. You. Speed?
	Silence.
	Anyone?
HARLEEN	I think – FAIZA – When you're driving to work –
ABZ	(*Pointedly at* HARLEEN.) Remember.
	FAIZA *duly raises her hand.*
FAIZA	When I'm on my way to the factory –
SAMIR	(*To* FAIZA.) You got a factory?
FAIZA	– I feel like I'm constantly telling people to move of out my way.
ABZ	Anyone else?
	HARLEEN *puts her hand up.*
	Go on.
HARLEEN	It's usually after a long shift in the hospital and I'm picking up my mum at rush hour, and people are driving like –
	dick–

ACT TWO, SCENE ONE   31

	– idiots. Then yes, sometimes I weave in and out of traffic –
ABZ	– You speed away from the hospital, you'll end up in it one day.
HARLEEN	That's a bit morbid.
FAIZA	God forbid.
ABZ	God, if he exists, will do all sorts of things if we lose our tempers.
SAMIR	Astaghfirullah.
	FAIZA *puts her hand up.*
ABZ	– Yes?
FAIZA	Music.
ABZ	Good, what is it about music?
FAIZA	I end up getting carried away.
	'Say you can't sleep, baby, I know, *That's that me espresso.'*
	SAMIR *sings along with* FAIZA *on the second lyric.*
SAMIR	Yo, that tune goes hard.
FAIZA	Before I know it, I'm doing sixty in a forty zone.
ABZ	Anyone else?
SAMIR	Raf-Saperra for me.
HARLEEN	(*To* SAMIR.) My go-to is Karan Aujla.
ABZ	That music is big part of the problem.
HARLEEN	Are you saying bhangra causes accidents?
SAMIR	(*To* HARLEEN.) My khala was caught in a ten-woman brawl after a Jazzy B concert.

ABZ	Whether we like it or not, there is a direct correlation between loud boom-bap anthems and reckless driving.
HARLEEN	Where are you even getting that from?
FAIZA	Does Sabrina Carpenter make boom-bap anthems?
ABZ	I want you all to try something next time you're in the car, turn on Classic FM for a change. See how that feels.
HARLEEN	I'll listen to what I want.
FAIZA	I think that's a great idea.
	ABZ *jots some notes down on the clipboard.* SAMIR *puts his hand up.*
ABZ	Yes Samir –
SAMIR	Yeah, Abzy. I don't think the issue is music –
ABZ	– It's JUST Abz. Not Abijit. Not Abishek. Not Abdullah. Just Abz. Is that clear?
SAMIR	Yeah... Sir.
	FAIZA *and* HARLEEN *try and stop themselves from laughing.*
ABZ	It's not getting through to any of you, is it?
SAMIR	What?
FAIZA	What are you writing, Mr Abz?
ABZ	Notes.
FAIZA	Am I –
	Are we doing well?
ABZ	Do you want the honest truth?
HARLEEN	That'd be helpful.
ABZ	You're in denial.

ACT TWO, SCENE ONE   33

He points at FAIZA.

You're trying to be the class clown.

He points at SAMIR.

And you're being antagonistic.

He points at HARLEEN.

FAIZA   I am not in denial.

SAMIR   I'm not a clown, bruv.

HARLEEN   I'm trying to engage, but you keep cutting me –

ABZ   – What are we good at as Brits?

FAIZA   Queuing.

SAMIR   Spying and shit –

             SAMIR *covers his mouth.*

HARLEEN   Bombing libraries and calling ourselves civilised.

ABZ   (*To* HARLEEN.) WRONG.

             (*To* FAIZA.) WRONG.

             (*To* SAMIR.) WRONG.

HARLEEN   What are we good at?

             ABZ *picks up his mug.*

ABZ   What does my mug say? It's the iconic World War Two slogan: *Keep calm and carry on.*

SAMIR   My mate sold them as aprons when the Queen died.

             ABZ *paces across the room frantically.*

ABZ   (*To* SAMIR.) Quiet.

             We kept calm. In the face of bombs. And we keep calm, whatever the challenges today.

	We're not out there rioting like the French over our pensions, are we?
	I'm seeing puzzled faces.
	What we're here to do today is firstly, to understand what happens to our bodies when we're enraged.
FAIZA	I get all clammy.
ABZ	Exactly Faiza. That can happen. But what about beforehand –
HARLEEN	– Something to do with adrenal glands in your body and –
ABZ	– Your body gets filled with stress hormones. All that blood in you is pumping toward your muscles preparing you for a battle.
HARLEEN	There's usually a reason though, no?
ABZ	We're human. We do let the outside world affect us. That's why you're all here. Seneca once said…
	ABZ gets frustrated by the fact that he's forgotten the quote.
	(*Under his breath.*) Fuck.
HARLEEN	(*To* FAIZA.) Did he just drop an F-bomb?
ABZ	Seneca once said…
	(*Under his breath.*) What was it?
SAMIR	You talking about the F1 driver who died?
ABZ	Shush. I've got it, I've got it.
	'Anger is more likely to do me more harm than your wrong.'

ACT TWO, SCENE ONE   35

HARLEEN	I don't really get it –
ABZ	– It's about learning to take the high road.
	...Especially this group.
HARLEEN	This group?
ABZ	Statistically, you're all susceptible to certain behaviours.
HARLEEN	Like what?
ABZ	Asian folks tend to be six to seven times more likely to be uninsured, especially in places like Birmingham, where we are right now.
SAMIR	(*To* HARLEEN.) It's called inshallah insurance.
HARLEEN	We're not the only ones getting in accidents though.
SAMIR	I'm insured but the amount I pay is a joke.
ABZ	What causes insurances rises? Car accidents. What causes car accidents? The number-one reason. Driver error or reaction. Where does that reaction stem from?
	Come on guys.
FAIZA	Anger. HARLEEN Anger
SAMIR	Anger.
ABZ	Exactly. And that is what R.U.N.D.I. is about. Unlearning and rehabilitating. Now it's time to get into your hidden selves.
	What is underneath your bonnet? What pressures. External pressures from our relationships, money problems, issues with your boss for example, can all change our mood in an instant –

SAMIR	– Pressure is for tyres.

ABZ *stares at* SAMIR.

Your brain is like an unruly horse. And you're the rider trying to get somewhere.

A hum begins to creep in. ABZ *notices a flicker of light in the ceiling, the Johari Window threatens to take over.* ABZ *quickly brings himself back to the present.*

So if you don't control what's going on in there, you're going to lose track.

This exercise is a tool to get those things out of our system. Does anyone know what these are?

ABZ *grabs some stress balls and attempts to juggle them.*

SAMIR	Balls.
ABZ	What kind?
HARLEEN	Stress balls?
ABZ	Bingo!

ABZ *throws a stress ball at* SAMIR.

How does it feel?

SAMIR	Nice and squeezy.
ABZ	What makes you angry? Give me something. Go on.
	Get up!
SAMIR	What?

SAMIR, FAIZA *and* HARLEEN *stand up.*

ABZ	Anything, c'mon.
SAMIR	Erm.

ACT TWO, SCENE ONE 37

ABZ	Throw it back.
	SAMIR *passes it to* ABZ.
	I'll start shall I: The DVLA. They lack innovation and it's infuriating.
	ABZ *squeezes the stress ball.*
HARLEEN	Don't you work for them?
ABZ	I'm setting the tone here. I want you to feel liberated to speak your mind. Go on, Samir.
	ABZ *throws the ball to* SAMIR *again.*
	Squeeze and release.
SAMIR	Okay.
ABZ	What makes you go ballistic?
SAMIR	Pot holes. Messes up my tyres, man.
	SAMIR *squeezes the stress ball.*
ABZ	Yes. Now throw it to Harleen.
	SAMIR *throws the ball to* HARLEEN.
HARLEEN	Parking tickets.
ABZ	Keep squeezing and pass it on.
	HARLEEN *to* FAIZA.
FAIZA	Lane-hoggers.
ABZ	Yes. YES.
	FAIZA *to* SAMIR.
SAMIR	When people don't tip after a delivery.
	SAMIR *to* FAIZA.
FAIZA	ULEZ. You've got to pay to breathe nowadays.
	FAIZA *to* HARLEEN.

HARLEEN	Barely having any money left after working all month.
ABZ	Yes, good.
	HARLEEN *to* SAMIR.
SAMIR	That jarring loop system in Leeds city centre.
	SAMIR *to* HARLEEN.
HARLEEN	Doctors who think they're the shit, when half the time I'm coming up with the same diagnosis.
	HARLEEN *to* FAIZA.
FAIZA	Small plates.
ABZ	Very specific.
	FAIZA *to* HARLEEN.
HARLEEN	If I see one more man – 'cause it's always a man – dash a Coke can out their car.
ABZ	It can be innocuous as littering, or it can be as big as climate change.
	HARLEEN *to* SAMIR.
SAMIR	Them BJP riots. Lost my mate 'cause of it.
HARLEEN	He died?
SAMIR	Nah, we fell out.
ABZ	Squeeze it, squeeze it.
SAMIR	That Dubai chocolate bar, it's all hype.
FAIZA	Marketing genius.
ABZ	Go further, come on.
	SAMIR *to* FAIZA.
FAIZA	Lazy people. This generation is full of them.
ABZ	YES. Put it ALL in the ball.

ACT TWO, SCENE ONE 39

FAIZA	I'm not ready to pass it on.
ABZ	Okay –
FAIZA	Twenty miles per hour zones.
ABZ	Important for safety, keep going!

FAIZA *to* HARLEEN.

HARLEEN The council in Brum refusing to pay bin men properly.

HARLEEN *to* SAMIR.

SAMIR The pigs harassing me.

ABZ *grimaces*. SAMIR *to* FAIZA.

FAIZA Average speed cameras.

ABZ Okay, they do save lives.

FAIZA *to* HARLEEN.

HARLEEN Evri dashing a parcel at my house like that Pakistani javelin thrower.

SAMIR (*To* HARLEEN.) I'd never dash a parcel.

HARLEEN *to* FAIZA.

FAIZA High tax and high inflation.

FAIZA *to* SAMIR.

SAMIR Imran Khan being locked up.

SAMIR *to* HARLEEN.

HARLEEN The fact that it's cheaper to fly to Spain than take the train to see my Masi in Liverpool.

HARLEEN *to* FAIZA.

FAIZA Electricity bills.

FAIZA *to* SAMIR.

ABZ Come on, Samir, what drives you crazy?

SAMIR	The genocide in Gaza.

ABZ takes the stress ball off SAMIR. A silence like the air has been sucked out of the room.

ABZ	Ahem. Alright alright, no politics.
SAMIR	– But it makes me angry.
ABZ	– Great, channel that. I want us to up the pace a little bit. It's anxiety hot potato. Feel it, squeeze it, release it!

ABZ throws the ball to HARLEEN.

HARLEEN	Men who lie.

HARLEEN to FAIZA.

FAIZA	Men who cheat.

FAIZA back to HARLEEN (they pass it to each other).

HARLEEN	Men in general.
FAIZA	Mummy's boys.
HARLEEN	Desi boys who don't know how to make roti, but expect you to know.
FAIZA	Asian boys driving like dickheads.
ABZ	Good.
HARLEEN	Boys trying to move to you at a gig.
FAIZA	Men who lie about their height.
ABZ	Can you feel the energy release!
SAMIR	HMRC. FAIZA Fucking HMRC.

ABZ hands each of them a stress ball to squeeze.

HARLEEN	My evil chacha. FAIZA Why's it always the –

ACT TWO, SCENE ONE   41

SAMIR	– Dad's side.
FAIZA	Being the middle child
HARLEEN	Being the eldest.
SAMIR	Youngest by ten years.
ABZ	Quicker. Faster.
SAMIR	When brothers take toe-to-toe in the mosque literally. My baby toe can't breathe, bruv.
FAIZA	Trying to secure a NADRA Card.
ABZ	Don't worry, just shout it out.
SAMIR	Chaiiwala falling off.
FAIZA	The oat milk industrial complex.
HARLEEN	Hustle culture.
SAMIR	No one's having house parties any more.

ABZ *gets into* SAMIR*'s face.*

ABZ	Let the stress flow out of you.
FAIZA	Constantly worrying about my little sister –
HARLEEN	Being gaslit by this country.
SAMIR	All these politicians.
FAIZA	All the fucking time.
ABZ	You're in control. YOU ARE IN CONTROL. Everything else, is just noise.

FAIZA *to* HARLEEN.

FAIZA	Patronising male CEOs who have small-dick energy.
HARLEEN	Being the family taxi driver.
SAMIR	Too many of my brother's having coke addictions.

FAIZA	Constantly getting belittled and undermined.
HARLEEN	Barely having a moment to myself.
FAIZA	Getting cheated out of 400k!
ABZ	EVERYBODY. STOP. This, this, is what we're here for.
	The unknown self!
	ABZ takes the stress ball from FAIZA.
	Faiza, go ahead.
FAIZA	I – um.
ABZ	Anything to share?
FAIZA	Well – about – erm –
ABZ	– Anything at all that relates to why you're here today.
FAIZA	That's okay, actually. That sort of –
	– came out of me.
ABZ	It's okay –
FAIZA	– Um, sure.
ABZ	– This is a safe space.
	FAIZA takes a moment.
FAIZA	Okay, I may have been involved in pursuing an ex-business partner.
HARLEEN	You got cheated out of 400k?
FAIZA	He cut me out the company I founded.
SAMIR	Was it fraud?
FAIZA	Not quite. Hostile takeover. Saudi guy, convinced me that his investment would upscale the whole operation.
SAMIR	What was the operation?

ACT TWO, SCENE ONE   43

FAIZA	– Hot-Girl-Henna, my hair-dye company.
HARLEEN	I think I've seen it sold in Sparkbrook.
ABZ	(*To* FAIZA.) – And in relation to the aggressive-driving incident –
FAIZA	– Yeah, sorry. Well, I saw him walking in Mayfair, getting into his car. This is after months of being stonewalled by his lawyers. And this man essentially crushed all my dreams. I had to remortgage my flat because of what he did. So when he saw me. He panicked.
HARLEEN	And then?
FAIZA	And then he ran. Well, drove away.
SAMIR	What a muppet.
FAIZA	So I did what any sane person would do.
ABZ	You followed him?
FAIZA	Abso-fucking-lutely.
SAMIR	What car did he drive?
FAIZA	A lime green Mustang.
HARLEEN	That's your first red flag.
SAMIR	What's your car?
FAIZA	BMW Coupé. Twenty-three plate.
SAMIR	Come in.
HARLEEN	– Go off.
ABZ	What did you do next, Faiza?
FAIZA	I did seventy on Edgware Road to catch him.
HARLEEN	In London?
FAIZA	Yep. He sees me following and has the gall to start breaking abruptly. We're now crawling

	on Park Lane and I'm horning non-stop. I eventually pull up beside him. I am ready.
HARLEEN	COME ON.
FAIZA	I open my window, he opens his. I'm ready to cuss his life out.
HARLEEN	Stop it.
FAIZA	And he says to me –
SAMIR	– What did he say?
FAIZA	– 'You're going to get hurt if you keep following me.'
HARLEEN	Threatening your life? After doing you dirty?
SAMIR	Oy, he's a proper harami.

ABZ *scribbles some notes on his clipboard.*

FAIZA	The lights go green. And he veers into my car and knocks my side mirrors CLEAN OFF. I'm in my element now.
	I weave through Park Lane overtaking everyone and anyone.
ABZ	These are several major traffic violations.
HARLEEN	Shush. SAMIR Shhh.
FAIZA	I'm determined to catch up. Then I see him, at the Park Lane roundabout. I mount this narrow curb and swerve right next to him. There are cars in front of him, he's got nowhere to go.
	I look at his face. And I feel sick. A handlebar moustache and Gucci glasses.
	I roll down my window. And I try to remember every swear word I know in Arabic.
	…And I say:

	'Kol Khara. El'an Abook. Telhaz Teeze. Sharmoot.'
	And I gather all the power I have in my body in that moment and swing my left arm to knock off his side-mirror. This Saudi boy is in complete shock.
HARLEEN	You deserve an award, sis.
SAMIR	What a badman.
FAIZA	Yes, he is.
	FAIZA *takes a deep breath.* ABZ *takes notes.*
ABZ	Faiza, how did you feel in the aftermath?
FAIZA	Righteous as fuck.
	Oh God, that was an F-bomb. Apologies.
HARLEEN	Can't think of a better feeling.
ABZ	Well done, Faiza. I know that was a lot.
FAIZA	The story isn't public knowledge.
ABZ	One of the most basic premises of the Johari Window is being open to sharing information about yourself.
FAIZA	I see.
ABZ	What we're building in this room is mutual trust.
	By the end of the day, I'd like you to take that trust onto the roads.
FAIZA	I would never think to do that again.
ABZ	Good, Faiza. It was unacceptable.
HARLEEN	I mean, a man did literally threaten her.
SAMIR	He defrauded her as well.

ABZ	Whatever he was going to say, Faiza had already erupted.

ABZ refers back to the Johari Window, he points at the 'Unknown' quadrant.

Because of the unknown. Hidden resentment. Hidden feelings brought to the surface –

ABZ is distracted by the hum and the flicker of the Johari Window threatens to enter. ABZ refocuses.

– by the stress ball so she's able to deal with it head on. And remember, you can fit one of these balls in your glove compartment.

ABZ throws FAIZA the stress ball.

We need to learn how to contain unknowns by sharing. So we can be 'zen', to use your words, Samir.

HARLEEN	(*To* FAIZA.) You did the right thing.
ABZ	No. She didn't. It's a slippery slope that takes someone from road rage to a prison cell.

Bring your chairs in everyone!

They all drag their chairs into the middle. ABZ stares at them all intensely.

This right here is called an assumption circle.

In our everyday lives, we feel like we can form an opinion about complete strangers. We all do it.

For this exercise, I want you all to imagine you saw each other on the road. For the very first time.

Only a glimpse. You might catch someone's facial expression, how they're dressed or the way they hold the steering wheel.

ACT TWO, SCENE ONE 47

> It could be anything.
>
> That's what I want you to do right now. To tell me what you think about each other. First impressions. It might feel awkward, you might get upset but judging is part of the exercise.

SAMIR Only God can judge me.

HARLEEN We barely know each other. I don't really want to judge someone else.

ABZ This is what I meant by meaningful engagement. Would you care to go first?

HARLEEN Fine.

ABZ Thank you.

> HARLEEN *tentatively stands up*.
>
> What assumption did you make about Harleen when she first walked in?

HARLEEN (*To herself.*) It's just awkward, standing in the middle –

ABZ Anyone?

FAIZA This is no disrespect.

ABZ Don't worry about adding caveats, Faiza.

FAIZA But when you walked in, you did have a distinctly annoyed demeanour.

HARLEEN Might have something to do with taking the day off work for this.

FAIZA Of course, I just wouldn't want to get into a slinging match with you on the road.

> HARLEEN *nods defiantly*.

ABZ You've gone quiet, Samir?

SAMIR	Erm. I-I-I'd notice her eyes first. And like the proper protective way she'd be steering. I'm guessing.
FAIZA	It wouldn't be a crash. It'd be a crush.
ABZ	Alright, alright that's enough of that, sit down.

HARLEEN *smiles and sits down.*

Faiza, could you stand please?

FAIZA *smiles and stands up.*

FAIZA	There really is no need.
ABZ	No need for what?
FAIZA	For me to do this. I've done a three-sixty process in every company I've run and the top three words that came back were visionary, inspirational and ethical.
ABZ	That's not what this exercise is, Faiza.
FAIZA	Oh.
ABZ	Any thoughts. Anyone?
HARLEEN	Girl-boss vibes.
FAIZA	Thank you.
ABZ	That's it? That's all you have?
	Samir?
SAMIR	You drive a Bimmer, right?
FAIZA	Yes. Coupé.
SAMIR	The Shadow edition goes crazy. What model you got?
FAIZA	The M8.
SAMIR	Are you serious? The M8?

ACT TWO, SCENE ONE   49

ABZ	What are your assumptions?
SAMIR	That's an 100k car. Biturbo as well. Jeez.
ABZ	Samir, FOCUS.
SAMIR	My bad, well, people who drive Beamers think they own the road.
FAIZA	(*Laughing.*) I don't think I own the road.
SAMIR	Leather steering wheel, yeah?
ABZ	(*Increasingly frustrated.*) Okay, forget it, Samir, stand up.
FAIZA	That's it?
	FAIZA *takes a seat.* SAMIR *stands up.*
ABZ	Any assumptions about Samir?
HARLEEN	He's got good posture.
	SAMIR *does an elaborate pec dance directing toward* HARLEEN.
SAMIR	Shoulders back.
ABZ	Faiza, any thoughts.
FAIZA	I do, yes.
ABZ	Go ahead.
FAIZA	I don't know if it's completely fair.
ABZ	That's what this exercise is about.
FAIZA	I don't know, I just –
ABZ	– Tell us, don't be shy.
FAIZA	Erm, well, there is a stereotype.
SAMIR	A stereotype?
ABZ	Tell us what the stereotype is.
FAIZA	– You know.

ABZ	No, I don't. Please share. Go with your gut.
FAIZA	I guess, the brown boy driving up and down Bury Park, eyeing up girls.
SAMIR	I'm not even from Luton. And I don't do that.
FAIZA	Well, it would be my first impression.

ABZ *makes notes on his clipboard.*

ABZ	Right, good, good, good. Keep going.
SAMIR	Keep going with what?
FAIZA	I don't know, it's your vibe, maybe –
SAMIR	My vibe?
FAIZA	You clearly love your cars and you probably race.
ABZ	He does.
FAIZA	I wouldn't be surprised if you've caused chaos on the roads.
ABZ	He probably has his silencer removed.
SAMIR	Woah, what is this, I'm want to sit down.
ABZ	You're not quite grappling what she's saying to you, Samir. Are you?
SAMIR	Nah, I fully understand it.
ABZ	(*To* FAIZA.) Clearly, he's a slow processor.
HARLEEN	That's out of order, that is.
SAMIR	What did you say?
ABZ	Calm down, it's an assumption.
	Samir, your nickname according to West Yorkshire police is Sammy the Raami. Faiza's assumption isn't without merit.

ACT TWO, SCENE ONE 51

SAMIR	First of all, it's pronounced, *Raami*. Secondly, we can just chat shit then?
ABZ	Watch your language.
SAMIR	What?
ABZ	'It is suspected that Samir Owais aka Pak Vin Diesel – a notorious local drag racer was travelling at one hundred and fifteen mph on the M4 in his Golf R.'
SAMIR	You don't the know the full story.
ABZ	You're right, but we need to understand the gap between perception and reality.
	Faiza made some assumptions. I shared some facts.
SAMIR	They're not facts.
ABZ	Okay, well, tell us the truth then.
SAMIR	I had to drive away quick.
ABZ	From who?
SAMIR	I don't even want to.
	SAMIR *sits back down*.
	ABZ *approaches* SAMIR
ABZ	Tell us, Samir.
HARLEEN	(*To* SAMIR.) What's he talking about?
SAMIR	I was chased, it wasn't even that deep.
	Silence.
	It was a bit of a situation, that's all.
ABZ	Where were you?
SAMIR	In Middlesborough, last summer.
ABZ	Something happened.

SAMIR	I went to get some milkshakes one night with my cousin, Waks.
ABZ	And?
SAMIR	A couple guys pulled up beside us, they said some things.
HARLEEN	What did they say?
SAMIR	It is what it is.
HARLEEN	It's okay, you can tell us.
	ABZ *offers a reassuring nod.*
SAMIR	The driver told me to wind down the window so I did. He says, 'Haven't you heard?' I said, 'What?' 'It's a purge for Pakis.'
	I said, 'What did you say?' They repeated it. 'It's the purge. We're hunting Pakis tonight.' Then they laughed.
HARLEEN	Samir, that's horrific.
SAMIR	Before I could even think to do anything, my cousin Waks dashed a milkshake in their faces.
	ABZ *grimaces.*
ABZ	You rose to the bait. Carry on.
	HARLEEN *stares down* ABZ.
SAMIR	I sped away, they followed us.
	We get to a red light, Waks looks at me like 'I guess we're gonna have to scrap these lot.' Two v four. Before Waks opens his door, I tell him to wait, the four of them come out and walk to our car, just as they get to the front doors, I put my foot down.
	I can see how pissed off they look in my rear-view mirror.

	Drenched in Daim bar and Lotus Biscoff milkshake.
	Waks has no idea that the only reason we survived is 'cause I read 'Ayatul Kursi' before we left.
HARLEEN	What dickheads.
FAIZA	I'm really sorry, Samir.
	ABZ *paces across the room.*
ABZ	Did you see how Faiza's assumptions, opened up something there?
SAMIR	It's just what happened.
	SAMIR *shrugs his shoulders.*
ABZ	As terrible as that event was, your blind spot is you weren't aware how you were perceived.
HARLEEN	(*To* ABZ.) How can that be your takeaway after what he shared?
ABZ	You're missing the point, Harleen.
HARLEEN	Which is what?
ABZ	We should accept that appearances matter to other road users.
	If we've got tinted windows, blasting loud music and have no respect for the law, we will be judged by that. It's human nature.
SAMIR	That's not even what I said.
ABZ	(*To* SAMIR.) Did this happen during the riots?
SAMIR	Yeah, I remember telling my mum to stay indoors for two weeks.
ABZ	You can't let isolated incidents, as horrible as they are, define you.

HARLEEN	They aren't isolated, what planet do you live on? I had cousins in Hull who had their door smashed in, it was like going back to the 1980s.
SAMIR	(*To* HARLEEN.) It was mad. The boys in Brum really came together. Sikh and Muslim. Alum Rock held it down.
ABZ	By reacting to their words, all you're doing is showing that you're being controlled by them.
SAMIR	Yeah, you throw a milkshake and keep it moving.
ABZ	No, you should've risen above it.
SAMIR	For who?
HARLEEN	He literally got racially abused?
ABZ	I am not disputing that.
HARLEEN	Have you looked in the mirror then? 'Cause if you were in that car, they'd have said exactly the same thing to you, Mr Abz.
ABZ	I am aware it's difficult.
HARLEEN	What would you do then?
ABZ	I wasn't there.
HARLEEN	If you were, what would you do?
ABZ	I'm not answering a hypothetical question. We're moving on.
HARLEEN	Answer the question?
FAIZA	Harleen, come on.
ABZ	Let's move on.
HARLEEN	I'm not moving on.
SAMIR	He doesn't even know himself.

ACT TWO, SCENE ONE

ABZ is distracted by the hum and the flicker of the Johari Window threatens to enter. ABZ *refocuses.*

ABZ — Fine, fine. You want to know what I'd do. I would take it on the chin, roll my window up and drive on.

HARLEEN — Take it on the chin?

ABZ — Wrong phrase, you get my point.

SAMIR — You'd let them hunt you down, calm.

HARLEEN — Take it on the chin. Understood. Loud and clear.

ABZ — I do not want you any of you to have criminal records, that's why we're here.

HARLEEN — Listen, if a Karen tries to make me feel small by even looking at me wrong, I'm out of my seat.

ABZ — And who would you be harming? You or Karen?

HARLEEN — I don't care if it's a double homicide, it's happening.

ABZ — (*Irritated.*) What I am sharing will make you calmer road users.

If you want to go, the door is right there. Just leave your licences on your way out.

Silence.

No?

Clearly, there is a lot of unlearning that needs to happen in this room.

(ABZ *points at* SAMIR.) When you feel that adrenaline, that cortisol reaching your head, you need to regulate your nervous system.

Do you know what the best medicine for your frustration is?

FAIZA *puts her hand up.*

(*To* FAIZA.) It's a rhetorical question. Guided meditation. Has anyone done this before?

Silence.

HARLEEN *rolls her eyes.*

Take your seats. Let's give it a go.

Close your eyes.

FAIZA *and* SAMIR *close their eyes.* HARLEEN *has one eye open.* ABZ *does too, eventually.*

Take a deep breath. Breathe in, breathe out.

In and out.

You're in your car seat, adjust your head and your neck.

Relax your shoulders, sink into the seat.

Let's clear some energy.

Inhale through the nose.

Expand your chest, exhale out with a sigh.

Now fill the body positive energy, with a renewed focus for the road ahead.

Your car is an energy bubble.

Holding you in its container.

An extension of your body, of your mind.

Notice your hands on the wheel.

Notice your feet on the floor and on the pedal.

ACT TWO, SCENE ONE 57

Notice your back on the seat.

Feel the air in your car, whether it's AC or the window down.

In this container, you're fully present and in control.

In this car, you're filled with a warm light.

Send all the negative thoughts out the back window.

Your only focus is your destination ahead.

Maybe another driver cut in front of you. Maybe a driver is on your bumper.

It doesn't matter.

Let the anxieties, stress and all feelings go.

ABZ phone starts to vibrate and he ignores it.

Whatever people say.

Whatever the world throws at you.

Whatever has happened in the past.

The hum returns and ABZ enters the Johari Window. The hum is coming from the kitchenette and gets louder and louder.

Let it go.

Keep breathing attentively.

Keep calm and drive safely.

ABZ walks toward the hum in an increasingly distressed state. He opens the kitchenette and stress balls pour out. He hastily puts them back.

ABZ returns to the present and everyone is where they were before in meditative practice.

	Coming back to the present moment.
	Until you reach your destination.
	Deep breaths everyone.
	And open your eyes.
	SAMIR, FAIZA *and* HARLEEN *open their eyes*. ABZ *buzzes again*.
	Let's take l-l-lunch.
SAMIR	Can you fix that vending machine?
ABZ	I'll go prep, stay seated.
	ABZ *exits*.

Scene Two

The conference room. HARLEEN *leans over to* FAIZA.

SAMIR	What the fuck was that?
HARLEEN	Keep your voice down FAIZA Shhh.
FAIZA	(*To* SAMIR.) You alright?
SAMIR	I'm fine, I'm fine. But he's moving mad. I think they're trying to stop us all from driving.
FAIZA	This is not some conspiracy, we just need to get through the day.
HARLEEN	Why does his phone keeping ringing?
	FAIZA *takes her phone out and waves it around to try and get signal.*
SAMIR	Look at us, we're all desi.

	FAIZA *takes her phone out and tries to hold it to the ceiling.*
	He doesn't want apneh on the roads.
FAIZA	He's Asian himself.
SAMIR	But they always send a brown person to do the white man's bidding, innit.
FAIZA	We are so close, so close –
HARLEEN	I do not trust that man.
	ABZ *re-enters with a sandwich tray, some disposable plates on a new sandwich cart and wheels it* SAMIR, FAIZA *and* HARLEEN.
ABZ	Sandwiches! Made them myself.
	Silence.
	Only kidding.
SAMIR	(*To* ABZ.) Is it protein?
ABZ	Cucumber.

They all sit in tense silence eating their sandwiches. All staring at each other with suspicion for some time.

ABZ *enters the Johari Window. The low frequency hum from the kitchenette shutters is getting louder and louder and louder.* ABZ *is startled and he walks toward it.* ABZ *returns to the present where* FAIZA, HARLEEN *and* SAMIR *are still eating their sandwiches.*

Scene Three

The conference room. ABZ wheels the sandwich cart away and returns to the group.

ABZ   A façade.

ABZ pauses.

A mask.

ABZ pauses again.

The hidden self can often be a defence mechanism. You know what you're hiding but you doing it for self-preservation.

ABZ refers to the Johari Window.

But when does your defence mechanism become something toxic on the road? When it rules you rather than you ruling it.

Well, you'll end up hitting, for example, a man on a moped just trying to do his job.

So how do we deal with that? How do we deal with conflict?

Anyone?

Silence.

This is exactly why we've got disorder on the streets.

De-escalation.

One way to practically look at de-escalating is… role play. Faiza, can you come forward please?

FAIZA   Sure.

ABZ   Anyone else want to volunteer?

ACT TWO, SCENE THREE

>SAMIR *stands up*.

>Thank you, Samir. Let's say, you're the CEO of a company.

FAIZA   I am an actual CEO.

ABZ   Yes, but for this role play, he's the CEO and you're the employee, Faiza. But you're not happy with him.

SAMIR   Why's she not happy with me?

ABZ   The scenario is that you, Samir, as her boss, have been stealing her ideas, pretending they were your ideas and giving her none of the credit. Faiza, your job is to talk to Samir as your boss and confront him. Let's go.

FAIZA   Shall I?

ABZ   – Go ahead.

FAIZA   Hello.

SAMIR   Time is money, what can I do for you?

FAIZA   Fine, let's cut to the chase, you're stealing my ideas.

SAMIR   Oh my bad, I didn't mean to.

ABZ   Okay, FREEZE.

>SAMIR *and* FAIZA *literally freeze*.

>I didn't mean literally.

>Samir, you're meant to be unsympathetic.

SAMIR   Like I don't care.

ABZ   Yes.

SAMIR   But I would care.

ABZ   Right, but it's a role play. Unfreeze, let's go.

SAMIR   Yeah, I stole your idea.

ABZ	No, FREEZE. Samir, you're not directly admitting to stealing her ideas.
SAMIR	I thought that's what I'm doing?
ABZ	No, no. Your perspective is that –
FAIZA	(*To* SAMIR) – You've got to *pretend* like you're not stealing my idea.
	Not that I would know anything about that.
SAMIR	Okay, I got you.
ABZ	(*Jaded*.) Let's go again.
FAIZA	Hi.
SAMIR	Yes.
FAIZA	You've stolen my idea and I've never been credited.
SAMIR	It's one company, one ummah. Your idea is my idea.
FAIZA	I'm just asking for my due credit.
SAMIR	I can't give it to you.
FAIZA	But you're presenting my ideas as your own.
SAMIR	I is we. That's my philosophy.
FAIZA	Oh gosh, I can feel the cortisol course through my body.
SAMIR	In fact. You're the one being selfish.
FAIZA	I can feel the release of the adrenaline.
SAMIR	You got no proof it's your idea I took, anyway.
FAIZA	I've got emails, hundreds of them, with proof of patents.
	Copyrights, witness statements, WhatsApps, thousands of them and even a recorded Zoom

	call. I could sue and if you didn't settle, I promise you that, as God is my witness, I will litigate your ass –
ABZ	– Okay, Faiza.
FAIZA	– LITIGATE YOUR ASS into bankruptcy –
	– but I won't. Because, flipping out will not result in changing the situation. Therefore I am not going to show any reaction or emotion.
SAMIR	(*Whispering to* FAIZA.) I see what you're doing, smart.
FAIZA	In fact, you might be an obnoxious boss and you might be judging me. But I am rising above it. I know you're simply trying to do your job and what's best for the company.
ABZ	Okay, good –
FAIZA	– So instead of getting angry, I'm going to thank you for taking my idea. Not only that, but I'm going to recommend that the you get awarded CEO of the year.
SAMIR	I appreciate that.
ABZ	Okay, nice U-turn there, Faiza. Let's swap it around. Faiza, you're the boss –
FAIZA	– My natural state
ABZ	– Samir, you're the employee, same scenario.
	Faiza, I'm going to need you to be more invested.
	Let's go.
SAMIR	You stole my idea for the company.
FAIZA	Don't flatter yourself.
SAMIR	I'm dead serious.

FAIZA	Why would I need to do that?
ABZ	Good.
SAMIR	If it wasn't for me, this company would be Asia Generic.
FAIZA	You do realise that's why I employee you, for your ideas.
ABZ	(*To* SAMIR.) How will you handle this, Samir?
SAMIR	(*To* ABZ.) I'm definitely feeling annoyed.
ABZ	Stick the knife in, Faiza.
FAIZA	Let's cut to the chase, we're all here to maximise shareholder profit. We're all cogs serving the machine and you, you grease the wheels so it can turn that little bit quicker.
SAMIR	I'm not WD-40. I'm a human being.
FAIZA	Don't get above your station.
SAMIR	That's harsh, that is.
FAIZA	Tough luck. Life's a bitch, ain't it.
SAMIR	Look. Even though I know you stole my idea, I could dispute it. But to quote Senna, getting vexed at you would hurt me so I'm not gonna do it.
FAIZA	How very emotionally mature of you. It sounds like you've studied the Johari Mirror –
	– Window.
ABZ	GOOD. What I am trying to help you learn is resilience. Embodying the Blitz Spirit and to take that into your driving.
	You can both go back.

	Now, let's do one more role play, maybe, car related.
	Harleen, let's say you're in your vehicle.
HARLEEN	Me?
ABZ	Come forward please.
HARLEEN	I'm alright, actually.
ABZ	Do I have to remind you about meaningful engagement?
HARLEEN	Fine.
	HARLEEN *stands up*.
ABZ	Let's say you're in a car park and I am a parking attendant.
HARLEEN	Why are you a parking attendant?
ABZ	Let's go.
	I'm afraid I've got to give you a ticket.
HARLEEN	Okay.
ABZ	Are you upset?
HARLEEN	No.
ABZ	Because we've got a zero tolerance policy on abuse.
HARLEEN	I've not abused you.
ABZ	I'm just doing my job like thousands of other –
HARLEEN	– I know you are.
ABZ	(*To* FAIZA *and* SAMIR.) She looks like she's going to lose it.
HARLEEN	(*Irritated.*) I've not lost it, have I?
ABZ	The mask you're wearing, it won't serve you.

HARLEEN	Are you still the parking attendant? Is this still the role play?
ABZ	Let's pause, relax Harleen, it's just an exercise. Let's say, in this scenario, we are at Wicksteed hospital on a Friday afternoon. Let's say, I wasn't being very kind to you.
	How would you react?
HARLEEN	I'd take it on the chin. Like you.
ABZ	In reality, would you have had, say, a violent outburst?
HARLEEN	I'm not doing this.
ABZ	Doing what? I'm asking questions.
HARLEEN	I've had it up to here, with you.
ABZ	Maybe even an act of aggression? Potentially GBH?
HARLEEN	That's not what happened.
ABZ	It's all here.
	ABZ refers to his clipboard.
HARLEEN	I parked. I paid. Finished a fourteen-hour shift where I had to clean up projectile vomit, two patients died on me and I got blamed for all of it. So when I forgot my coat at the hospital and ran back to my car and saw that I got a ticket, after all of that?
	Yeah, I blew up a little.
ABZ	You threatened to ram a parking attendant with your Vauxhall Corsa.
HARLEEN	You're twisting things –
ABZ	– Before chasing them as they got on their moped –

ACT TWO, SCENE THREE 67

HARLEEN — I didn't actually do it though, did I? Did I?

ABZ As I said, a violent threat, that's a criminal offence.

HARLEEN And all I actually did was horn at him.

ABZ And all I'm trying to help you, so you don't make random threats to people on the road.

HARLEEN You're telling us to swallow disrespect? I will follow a man to his yard and fuck shit up if I have to.

ABZ phone rings.

ABZ Let's stop for a moment.

ABZ leaves the conference room. HARLEEN *heads for the door.*

FAIZA Where are you going?

SAMIR Are you good?

HARLEEN I think I'm done.

FAIZA Done with this?

HARLEEN I'll wake up two hours earlier if I have to, I'll take three buses and I'll sacrifice night shifts. But I am done with this shit.

FAIZA What if all we get banned because of you?

HARLEEN I need to do what I need to.

FAIZA How selfish.

HARLEEN Yeah, for once in my life.

FAIZA Okay, okay, you can't leave yet until I try to find out what happens to us. I'm going to contact someone at the DVLA and get an answer. Hold your horses.

FAIZA takes her phone out and stands on a chair.

HARLEEN	What the hell are you doing?
FAIZA	There's got to be signal somewhere

FAIZA *waves her phone at the ceiling.*

SAMIR	Come on.
FAIZA	OH MY GOSH. I'M BACK ON THE CAFFÉ NERO WI-FI.

FAIZA *checks her emails.*

FUCK.

SAMIR	WHAT?
FAIZA	The fucking Indonesians didn't go for it.
HARLEEN	What?
FAIZA	The deal, my fucking business deal.
SAMIR	(*To* FAIZA.) You could try the Malaysians?

ABZ *returns looking even more disturbed.*

ABZ	What in the world is going on here?
HARLEEN	She um –
FAIZA	One second.
ABZ	Get down now!
FAIZA	Yep, hold on
ABZ	I TOLD YOU, GET DOWN.
	Are we ready to finish this exercise?
FAIZA	Yes.
ABZ	Good.

They all nod. FAIZA *glances at her phone.*

FAIZA	Oh my gosh.
ABZ	What now, Faiza?

ACT TWO, SCENE THREE 69

FAIZA	I've got an email from the DVLA.
ABZ	Give me your phone.
FAIZA	Saying the session was cancelled?

Silence.

ABZ	That's not true. Let's carry on.

FAIZA *walks over to* HARLEEN.

FAIZA	Have a look at this.
ABZ	It's a mistake, are you hearing me?

HARLEEN *takes* FAIZA*'s phone.*

HARLEEN	'Urgent: please note your Rehabilitating and Unlearning, National Driving Initiative course has been cancelled. We apologise for the short notice. Please await further instruction from the Driving and Licensing Agency.'
ABZ	How can it be cancelled? We're in the middle of the session.
SAMIR	What is going on? Is this meant to be happening or not?
FAIZA	Good question.
ABZ	They wouldn't cancel the session while it's in motion.
HARLEEN	Why do you keep leaving?
FAIZA	And you told me I can't leave the room.
ABZ	The email. It's probably been accidentally sent to the wrong person. That's all.
SAMIR	But you said we're the first ones to do it?
HARLEEN	You need to prove who you say you are, that's what you need to do.

ABZ	I will not respond to intimidation, Harleen.
HARLEEN	I don't care, okay. I don't care any more. I just want to leave.

ABZ is simmering.

ABZ	We're almost there, we're expanding your arenas, cracking your masks open and interrogating your blind spots. Then you'll be ready and safe to be on the road and maintain your licences.
FAIZA	So we are getting our licences?
ABZ	Only if you complete the course.
HARLEEN	If the email is a mistake, like you say it is, show us the proof.
ABZ	I am not required to. Now, take a seat.
SAMIR	We need to know, for safety reasons. You could be doing fraud. Charging us to sit here and waffle.
ABZ	Safety? I've told you who I am.
FAIZA	We're in a basement with a stranger who said we can't leave the building and then I get this email. It's absolutely about safety.
SAMIR	Start talking, Mr Abz.
ABZ	Is that meant to be a threat?
SAMIR	If you want to take it that way.
HARLEEN	What he's trying to say is none of this makes sense. You need to make it make sense or I'm leaving.
ABZ	You've had all the official correspondence, you're so close, don't throw it all away.
HARLEEN	Sod this, I'm done.

	HARLEEN *heads for the door.* ABZ *blocks the entrance to the break room.*
ABZ	No. No. Stop behaving like irrational children.
HARLEEN	Move out my way.
ABZ	I'm not giving up on you.
SAMIR	Oi, you better move.
HARLEEN	Are you stupid? Unlock the door, I'll slap you round the head.
ABZ	We've got one more exercise –
SAMIR	– No one gives a shit about your exercises.
	ABZ *explodes in anger.*
ABZ	THIS RIGHT HERE, WHAT WE'RE DOING, IT'S BIGGER THAN WHAT YOUR LITTLE BRAINS CAN EVEN CONCEIVE OF. THIS WILL SAVE YOUR LIFE. SAVE THE LIFE OF OTHERS AROUND YOU.
	SAMIR *stands up.* HARLEEN *steps back.*
SAMIR	I told you, they're tryna stop apneh from driving! Didn't I say it?
ABZ	You do understand this isn't just about the fucking course?
	ABZ *tries to calm himself down and escape the Johari Window.*
	Now let's all take a big deep breath and countdown from ten.
FAIZA	Oh fuck off with your fucking countdowns.
SAMIR	I'll handle this.
HARLEEN	Handle what? Leave it, Samir.

SAMIR	Move.
ABZ	I am going to start the countdown.
	Don't act like an animal, Samir.
	ABZ notices hum and flicker of the Johari Window starts to creep in and build slowly through the scene. SAMIR tries to walk past ABZ but blocks his path. They square up.
SAMIR	What the fuck are you doing?
FAIZA	I can't watch.
ABZ	Deep breath, ten.
SAMIR	This is your last warning.
ABZ	Don't let your base self-dominate. Nine.
SAMIR	I'll break your fucking hand.
ABZ	Let your breath guide you. Eight.
FAIZA	I think I have low blood sugar.
SAMIR	Are you tapped in the head?
ABZ	SEVEN.
	SAMIR tries to push past again, ABZ puts his arm out.
HARLEEN	SAMIR, STOP.
ABZ	SIX.
HARLEEN	STOP IT.
ABZ	Don't feed into your inner impulses, Samir.
	FIVE.
SAMIR	You got five seconds to move before you feel my inner impulse.
ABZ	FOUR.
FAIZA	I don't feel right about any of this.

ACT TWO, SCENE THREE

>FAIZA *holds onto a chair to keep her balance.*

ABZ THREE.

>SAMIR *tries to walk past again but* ABZ *grabs his arm and twists it as if he's arresting him.*

You don't know what's good for you, do you? You silly, silly boy.

SAMIR Oi, stop, fuck, my arm?!

HARLEEN YOU'RE HURTING HIM?

>ABZ *pushes* SAMIR *back.*

ABZ Do you see how dangerous you're when you're all out of control? Do you see that?

ONE. Are we all calm? How do we feel?

>FAIZA *starts to sob.*

SAMIR YOU FUCKED IT NOW.

>SAMIR *runs to 'spear'* ABZ *who anticipates it and puts him in a headlock. The two of them start wrestling.*

HARLEEN Samir, NO!

ABZ How'd you like that, boy racer?

FAIZA (*In tears.*) WHAT THE HELL ARE YOU DOING?

>SAMIR *and* ABZ *grapple with each other.* HARLEEN *scans the room.* FAIZA *is trying to make a call on her phone.*

SAMIR FIGHT ME FAIRLY, YOU PRICK.

ABZ I didn't want to have to do this. You forced me. You forced me.

>FAIZA *screams and jumps on* ABZ's *back.*

>   HARLEEN *walks over to the desk and grabs the 'KEEP CALM AND CARRY ON' mug. She walks slowly behind* ABZ.
>
>   FAIZA, SAMIR *and* ABZ *are now all embroiled in a brawl.*

HARLEEN   MOVE.

>   ABZ *enters the Johari Window as* HARLEEN's *winds her arm back with the mug in her hand.*
>
>   ABZ *returns to the present, again.* HARLEEN *smashes the mug on* ABZ's *head and knocks him out.*

ACT THREE

Scene One

ABZ is unconscious on the floor with a pool of blood around him. There is silence. FAIZA is in a state of shock, SAMIR is pacing around the room and HARLEEN is frozen.

FAIZA	Fuck. Fuck. Fuck. I'm going to prison. I am absolutely going to prison for this.
SAMIR	Oy, oy, oy.
FAIZA	Oh God, there's blood pouring out. That's BLOOD.
SAMIR	What. Happened?
	HARLEEN *takes a deep breath.*
FAIZA	Does anyone know what prison is like?
	FAIZA *looks at* SAMIR.
SAMIR	Why are you looking at me?
FAIZA	Because we have killed a man. She has killed a man.
	HARLEEN *goes to the break-room area.*
SAMIR	It's not her fault.
FAIZA	Well, he's dead isn't he? WHERE IS SHE GOING?
	(*To* HARLEEN.) WHERE ARE YOU GOING?
	HARLEEN *searches the break-room area for a first aid kit.* FAIZA *follows her.*
	If you're thinking of running, I'll run after you. I-I'll tackle you to the floor.

	HARLEEN *stares back at her.*
	Okay, maybe not.
	Meanwhile, SAMIR crouches down to touch ABZ's neck.
	HARLEEN returns with a first aid kit in her hand and a wet cloth. FAIZA follows.
	SAMIR looks up and shakes his head.
SAMIR	He's dead. Gone. Finito.
FAIZA	Oh my God.
	FAIZA screams.
SAMIR	Inna Lillahi wa inna ilahi raji-un.
	HARLEEN crouches down and checks his pulse.
HARLEEN	He's not dead.
FAIZA	He's not?
HARLEEN	I hit him on the hard part of the head.
	SAMIR touches his forehead.
	HARLEEN applies a wet cloth to his head. She opens the first aid kit and takes out a bandage. She turns ABZ to one side and starts putting a bandage round his head.
	He's breathing fine.
FAIZA	(*To* SAMIR.) What fucking pulse were you checking for?
SAMIR	Near his chin.
	HARLEEN takes another deep breath.
HARLEEN	What do we now?
SAMIR	I dunno.

ACT THREE, SCENE ONE   77

FAIZA	Call the police?
SAMIR	No way. HARLEEN No.
FAIZA	Why not?
SAMIR	They'll arrest the three of us for assault.
FAIZA	What do you suggest?
HARLEEN	Hurry up, he's waking up.

ABZ shakes his head gingerly.

ABZ	Oh God.
HARLEEN	I've got it.
SAMIR	What?
HARLEEN	If we could find –
SAMIR	Say it in another language.

SAMIR tries to subtly point at FAIZA.

FAIZA	No, no, let's speak English here.
SAMIR	Ki chai'da ae?
HARLEEN	Kuch vi. Fuck. How do you say it.
SAMIR	What? What?
HARLEEN	Anu banhan nu kuch chai'da ae.
FAIZA	What are you language are you speaking?
SAMIR	Rope?
FAIZA	ROPE? What you going to do with ROPE?
HARLEEN	Because he's dangerous. Shit. Go, go, go.
	He frantically searches through the kitchenette.
	ABZ starts to groan.
	HURRY!

FAIZA	I AM NOT INVOLVED.

He takes the table cloth and turns it into a make-shift rope and hands it to HARLEEN.

IF THE MI5 ARE LISTENING, I AM NOT INVOLVED IN WHATEVER THEY ARE DOING.

HARLEEN	It was self-defence.
SAMIR	(*To* HARLEEN.) I'd have handled him.
FAIZA	(*To* SAMIR.) You wouldn't have handled him.
	(*To* HARLEEN.) I told you to chillax and you went and smashed him with a mug.
HARLEEN	Can I remind you, Faiza, that you jumped on the man's back?
FAIZA	He had Samir in a headlock.
SAMIR	I was about to throw him over my head.
HARLEEN	We all made choices.

HARLEEN *tries to bind* ABZ's *hands.*

FAIZA	Not only have you beaten a man, but you are now planning to take him hostage.
HARLEEN	Temporary restraint.
SAMIR	He was trying to lock us in here.
FAIZA	We don't know that. I think this was disproportionate.
HARLEEN	You were shouting for him to move just like we were.
FAIZA	Yes, yes, I was. That really doesn't explain why we are tying him up.
HARLEEN	To ask him what his plan was.

FAIZA	Yes, I'm at my most understanding when I'm gagged and bound, makes sense.
HARLEEN	(*To* SAMIR.) Go grab something to put in his mouth.
FAIZA	(*To* SAMIR.) Why are you following her instructions like a lapdog?
	SAMIR *runs to the break-room area.*
	I actually can't do this. I'm going. And you can't stop me.
	FAIZA *stands to leave.*
HARLEEN	We'll tell the police you were involved.
FAIZA	You wouldn't dare.
HARLEEN	You were the one dragging him off, Samir.
FAIZA	You'd seriously blackmail me?
HARLEEN	Faiza, please. One thing at a time.
	FAIZA *sits back down.* SAMIR *returns with a cloth.*
SAMIR	Found it.
HARLEEN	(*To* SAMIR.) Give me a hand.
	SAMIR *walks over and they lift* ABZ *up onto the chair. They both take a moment.*
FAIZA	I can't do this.
	SAMIR *walks over to pick up a stress ball and throws it at* FAIZA.
	What am I meant to do with this?
SAMIR	Squeeze it and release.
FAIZA	I'm not going to fucking squeeze it.
	ABZ *is groggily shaking his head.*

SAMIR	What do we do?
HARLEEN	We should explain that it –
SAMIR	– Yeah?
HARLEEN	– It all got out of control.
FAIZA	I was building generational wealth.
HARLEEN	Maybe grab some water. We can pour some on his head.
	SAMIR *heads to the break room, grabs two glasses of water.*
FAIZA	What are you gonna do, interrogate him?
	SAMIR *enters the conference room with two glasses of water, he hands one to* HARLEEN.
	HARLEEN *throws the water on* ABZ*'s face. He's shakes his head and starts to talk.*
ABZ	It's coming for me. It's coming. The shadows.
HARLEEN	Who is?
ABZ	The unknowns.
SAMIR	What unknown?
HARLEEN	He's hallucinating.
ABZ	The known unknowns.
SAMIR	He sounds like my uncle who chews khat.
HARLEEN	(*To* FAIZA.) Mr Abz. Do not panic. Do not panic.
FAIZA	I WANT TO CLARIFY FOR THE RECORD, I HAVE NOTHING TO DO WITH THIS.
HARLEEN	Can you stop shouting in his face?
ABZ	Go away, go away. Go away.
FAIZA	(*To* HARLEEN.) Why is he talking like that?

HARLEEN	My guess would be mild aphasia after a concussion.
FAIZA	What is that? Brain damage?
HARLEEN	Communication issues. It's normal. That's normal.

ABZ passes out. HARLEEN moves closer to ABZ to check he's okay.

HARLEEN kneels next to ABZ. He jolts awake and they all take a step back.

ABZ	W-W-WHAT, WHERE AM I?
HARLEEN	Relax, Abz. Just relax.
ABZ	W-W-WHY AM I TIED UP?
SAMIR	We got a couple of questions.
FAIZA	(*To* SAMIR.) That's not helpful.
ABZ	I'LL SCREAM.

HARLEEN grabs the cloth off SAMIR and gags ABZ who tries to scream through it.

FAIZA	Well, this is going well.
SAMIR	CALM DOWN. OKAY. CALM IT.
HARLEEN	Stop screaming, okay. Stop. You were bleeding.

ABZ tires himself out. SAMIR looks at HARLEEN and she nods to take the cloth out of his mouth.

ABZ	WHAT THE FUCK ARE YOU DOING?
HARLEEN	Mr Abz, relax. Alright? Relax. We're going to untie you.
ABZ	WELL FUCKING DO IT THEN.
HARLEEN	If you scream again, we'll gag you.

ABZ	OKAY. OKAY. OKAY. UNTIE ME AND WE CAN TALK.
HARLEEN	We don't feel safe enough to do that yet.
ABZ	SAFE? I'M AN ACCREDITED DVLA INSTRUCTOR.
HARLEEN	We can't trust that.
FAIZA	Stop saying 'we'.
ABZ	Y-YOU ATTACKED ME.
HARLEEN	You had him in a headlock.
SAMIR	Took me by surprise.
	ABZ *takes a moment.*
HARLEEN	You need to tell us who you are.
ABZ	You've made a big mistake here.
HARLEEN	What are we doing here, Abz?
ABZ	There's no coming back from this.
	SAMIR *fishes* ABZ*'s phone out of his pocket.*
	What are you doing?
	That is my personal property.
SAMIR	Got it.
ABZ	THEFT. YOU'RE A THEIF.
HARLEEN	Check the call log?
	SAMIR *puts* ABZ *phone to his face to unlock his phone ID. He tries to turn away.*
SAMIR	Who is DVLA Dave and why's he called you eight times?
ABZ	He is –
	He's a colleague.

HARLEEN	What did he say to you?
ABZ	He-he-he was asking how it's going.
	FAIZA *walks over and grabs his clipboard.*
SAMIR	What does that say?
FAIZA	'FA has delusions of grandeur, aloof.'
HARLEEN	FA?
FAIZA	My initials.
HARLEEN	What else?
FAIZA	'SO – unaware of how he appears as a driver. A TP boy-racer. Needs reform.'
	What's TP?
SAMIR	Typical Paki.
HARLEEN	(*To* ABZ.) You kuttah.
ABZ	Those are private notes.
FAIZA	'HK, hugely guarded. Victim mentality.
	Clear chip on shoulder.'
FAIZA	Okay, he could *actually* be a psycho.
ABZ	I've got all your records on the DVLA system. I'm telling you –
	The pilot –
	– the scheme, it's legitimate. Totally legitimate.
HARLEEN	I'm going to go and get help.
	HARLEEN *heads to the exit.*
ABZ	No-no. No no. No need to do all of that.
	HOLD ON. Okay. The DVLA decided to scrap R.U.N.D.I.

FAIZA	When?
ABZ	Today. They said that the new CEO said it's a waste of money and the decision is immediate. They didn't care I was in the middle of the session.
HARLEEN	You knew it was cancelled?
SAMIR	You said all the stuff about nine points and how if we took part –
ABZ	– That was true. Honest to God. This is all years of planning.
	I'd got permission months in advance but then they rang –
HARLEEN	– Dave rang you.
ABZ	He tried this morning, they couldn't get through.
	ABZ nods. It dawns on SAMIR that he might not keep his licence.
HARLEEN	So they told you that they're not doing this stupid scheme any more, you what, you just kept us here?
FAIZA	Without telling us?
	ABZ is silent.
	That was a question?
ABZ	Yes. They said I should let you go, the scheme had its funding pulled.
HARLEEN	But you still made notes on us?
SAMIR	Have we still got our licences?
ABZ	I don't know.
SAMIR	Nah, I'm not playing.
ABZ	I don't know about your licences, okay.

SAMIR	That's my livelihood. I need an answer.
ABZ	Part of the terms of attending this, would be you'd avoid the points. I'm guessing because it's cancelled that you've…
FAIZA	…Lost our licences. Great.
SAMIR	You do realise, I can't go without it. You better do something.
ABZ	There's nothing I can do.
SAMIR	You fucking led us on the whole day, text your boss now.
	Tell him you done something illegal, so we all need to keep our licences.
	SAMIR *walks over to untie* ABZ.
	I'll untie you, you'll need to text him now.
HARLEEN	(*To* SAMIR.) Samir, Samir. Take it easy.
	HARLEEN *holds* SAMIR*'s arm.*
ABZ	Maybe you shouldn't have got angry and sped away in your car.
SAMIR	Oh you're going to get it.
	HARLEEN *holds* SAMIR *back.*
HARLEEN	Look at me, don't let him get into your head.
	SAMIR *walks over to grab a glass of water.*
ABZ	You've all proved my point. You let yourself be drawn into becoming your base selves. What you probably do on the roads, day after day. I tried to stupidly reign you all in. Save you. And you all failed.
HARLEEN	Oh shut up.
ABZ	You all disgust me.

SAMIR throws the glass of water on ABZ's face.

Why'd you do that?

FAIZA   Samir?

SAMIR   It's what they did in Guantanamo.

ABZ   That's not what waterboarding is, you idiot.

SAMIR   Firstly, I'm not an idiot. Secondly, why do you speed?

Why do you speed? Huh? Why do you SPEED?

ABZ   I don't. Because I know the consequences.

SAMIR   What is it? What's the reason? For the thrill of it?

ABZ   The things I've seen, you wouldn't even know.

SAMIR   WHY DO YOU SPEED? It's pretty simple question.

ABZ   I-I-I don't speed. I teach *speed* awareness.

SAMIR   WRONG.

FAIZA picks up a stress ball and throws it at ABZ's head.

FAIZA   Give us your external pressures, go on.

ABZ   Ouch.

FAIZA picks up another stress ball and throws it at ABZ's head.

FAIZA   Go on, tell us. What are they?

What makes you angry?

FAIZA picks up a stress ball and throws it at ABZ's head.

ACT THREE, SCENE ONE

ABZ	I'm reforming your aggression. Everything I taught you is foolproof.
FAIZA	SQUEEZE AND RELEASE!
ABZ	Because I know this works.
FAIZA	Let it wash over you.

FAIZA *picks up a stress ball and throws it at* ABZ*'s head.*

HARLEEN	What assumptions have we got about him?
SAMIR	Probably drives a Toyota Prius.
ABZ	I know my blind spots. Don't try me.
FAIZA	Definitely lives alone.
SAMIR	I bet he doesn't have a missus.
ABZ	(*To himself.*) Stay composed.
HARLEEN	Well, let's do a role play. Let's say I'm the DVLA boss cancelling your course.
ABZ	I refuse –
HARLEEN	– Ring, ring, I'm calling you thirty times to tell you to release the strangers in the hotel basement.

ABZ *starts to hyperventilate.*

ABZ	That's not what I was doing.
HARLEEN	Fundamentally, Abz, this whole R.U.N.D.I. programme is a load of bollocks.
ABZ	Don't you dare –
HARLEEN	– It's helped no one, how about that?
ABZ	– It helped me. It saved me.
HARLEEN	How did you react to that, Mr Abz?
ABZ	You have no clue, no clue.

HARLEEN	Did you de-escalate, or did you keep your mask on? Or did you snap into pieces?
ABZ	(*Snaps.*) Do you even know what I've had to deal with to get here?! I had bury my own wife because of what I did.
	Silence.
FAIZA	What did you do?
ABZ	It was an accident –
	– It was a car accident –
	– It doesn't matter.
SAMIR	An accident? Where?
	ABZ *looks away.*
	Do I have to repeat myself?
ABZ	I can't.
HARLEEN	We are in way too deep to turn back now.
ABZ	Near the Bingley bypass.
SAMIR	I know it.
	Silence.
HARLEEN	We're either leaving you here tied up or you speak –
ABZ	– It was, it was –
	– this driver behind me. Back when I used to race.
SAMIR	Racing? Are you taking the piss?
HARLEEN	Samir, let him finish.
ABZ	This was a lifetime ago, okay. I didn't intend to. He overtook me and started swerving across lanes.

	I got in front, and the other guy, he didn't seem to like that very much. I start breaking abruptly and he swings to the side of me, opens the window and spits at us.
FAIZA	Us?
ABZ	Mariam. Me and Mariam. He spat at her. I could see her in shock. I-I-I reacted. A red mist came over me. I put my foot to the pedal.

ABZ *voice breaks*.

The road – the road is going two into one. Two into one.

I got in front. I can see he's rattled. So he pulls up to the left of me, forces me into the opposite lane.

We are neck and neck... Mariam is shouting at me. Screaming. Telling me to relax.

I glanced to take a look at him and then something strange happened... She tells me to slam the breaks and all I see is blinding lights. A lorry charging toward me.

ABZ *takes a moment, he's at breaking point*.

Everything was a blur... and then I blacked out.

A loud crash.

HARLEEN	When was this?
	ABZ *is in tears*.
ABZ	Seven years ago, today.
	She told me to take it easy. She told me –
SAMIR	– This was your wife?
	Silence.
	It's like I'm haunted by it.

FAIZA	That's dreadful.
ABZ	If I could save one person from doing what I did.
HARLEEN	– We didn't have a choice in that though, did we?
ABZ	– I had to beg the DVLA to let me run this.
SAMIR	– How do you even work for them?
FAIZA	You're their poster child for rehabilitation.
HARLEEN	Why did they really cancel it?
ABZ	They thought it might look bad.
FAIZA	What would?
ABZ	They thought it could like we're racially profiling people –
SAMIR	– I knew it!
HARLEEN	– That's exactly why you're doing.
ABZ	No, I chose you all, because I want us to do better.
FAIZA	You chose us?
HARLEEN	Us? So now it's 'us'?
ABZ	You all need to wake up.
HARLEEN	You think you see us, but you really don't.
ABZ	We're getting battered out there.
	Do you think losing control in the way that you have does anything but reinforce harmful stereotypes about us?
SAMIR	From who?
ABZ	Because all they would see if they walked in this room is a bunch of –

SAMIR	– Don't.
ABZ	I know you don't like it, but I am here to help you.
FAIZA	How exactly are you helping? I'm sorry, but you can't save us with a diagram you found off the internet. And you can't break people up into pieces. Brown, angry or hidden.

Whatever self you're looking at – you're not a window.

You're a person. |
| ABZ | You're not getting it. Nobody, I mean nobody is going to tell you how it is. But I am. Believe me, all your rage will do is destroy you and everyone we love. |
| HARLEEN | Everyone I love –

– I look at my nani and I wonder if we were better off in her pind. Because we all do is we give and we give and we give and we get spat back out and told to be grateful. Then we get you telling us to 'keep calm and carry on'. It's like we're the only ones being told to hold ourselves back. I'm not doing that. |
ABZ	Fine, if you really don't want my help, carry on. You'll see.
SAMIR	You decided who I was before I walked in. Maybe you don't like me 'cause when you look at me, you see yourself. But I'm nothing like you.
ABZ	You are to them.
HARLEEN	We're not the ones that need help, you do. And everything you're doing is feeding that system and making it worse.

A brief silence.

FAIZA	I hope you can forgive yourself, Abz.
	SAMIR, FAIZA *and* HARLEEN *look at* ABZ *with pity.*
ABZ	Don't look at me like that.
HARLEEN	Have you got someone you can call?
ABZ	No.
HARLEEN	Well, you'll need to get your head checked out then.
	FAIZA *walks over to unties* ABZ*'s arms but not his hands.*
FAIZA	Keys.
	ABZ *hands her the keys to the door.*
	HARLEEN *and* FAIZA *start to walk out,* SAMIR *joins them.*
ABZ	Are you just going to walk out? I've invested my time in you. If you want, bail. Go ahead. Go. See if I care. You had all these opportunities to improve, to change. But you've fucked it. Haven't you?
	In the break-room area, a Rubicon Mango comes out of the vending machine. SAMIR *picks it up and walks toward* ABZ.
	You had your chance, this is what it is. That's it now. Because you lost it. You lost your head. And there is no coming back from this. Go on, say something. Say something. You're useless, you're pathetic. Come on then, have a swing.

Look at me. Look at me.

SAMIR *puts the can down.* ABZ *pauses.*

Don't go. Please don't go.
Please.
Don't go.

SAMIR, FAIZA *and* HARLEEN *leave.*

ABZ *is left alone, in silence with nothing but the humming of the basement. Isolated in his grief. He stands and picks up the bouquet of flowers on the table.*

The End.

A Nick Hern Book

Speed first published in Great Britain in 2025 as a paperback original by Nick Hern Books Limited, The Glasshouse, 49a Goldhawk Road, London W12 8QP, in association with the Bush Theatre, London

Speed copyright © 2025 Mohamed-Zain Dada

Mohamed-Zain Dada has asserted his moral right to be identified as the author of this work

Cover image: Maskot / Alamy Stock Photo

Designed and typeset by Nick Hern Books, London
Printed in the UK by Mimeo Ltd, Huntingdon, Cambridgeshire PE29 6XX

A CIP catalogue record for this book is available from the British Library

ISBN 978 1 83904 471 7

CAUTION All rights whatsoever in this play are strictly reserved. Requests to reproduce the text in whole or in part should be addressed to the publisher.

Amateur Performing Rights Applications for performance, including readings and excerpts, by amateurs in the English language throughout the world should be addressed to the Performing Rights Department, Nick Hern Books, The Glasshouse, 49a Goldhawk Road, London W12 8QP, *tel* +44 (0)20 8749 4953, *email* rights@nickhernbooks.co.uk, except as follows:

Australia: ORiGiN Theatrical, Level 1, 213 Clarence Street, Sydney NSW 2000, *tel* +61 (2) 8514 5201, *email* enquiries@originmusic.com.au, *web* www.origintheatrical.com.au

New Zealand: Play Bureau, 20 Rua Street, Mangapapa, Gisborne, 4010, *tel* +64 21 258 3998, *email* info@playbureau.com

United States and Canada: Casarotto Ramsay and Associates Ltd, see details below

Professional Performing Rights Applications for performance by professionals in any medium and in any language throughout the world (including by stock companies in the USA and Canada) should be addressed to Casarotto Ramsay and Associates Ltd, *email* rights@casarotto.co.uk, www.casarotto.co.uk

No performance of any kind may be given unless a licence has been obtained. Applications should be made before rehearsals begin. Publication of this play does not necessarily indicate its availability for amateur performance.

www.nickhernbooks.co.uk/environmental-policy

Nick Hern Books' authorised representative in the EU is
Easy Access System Europe – Mustamäe tee 50, 10621 Tallinn, Estonia
email gpsr.requests@easproject.com

www.nickhernbooks.co.uk

@nickhernbooks